COCKTAIL
aficionado

COCKTAIL
aficionado

Allan Gage

MQP

An Hachette Livre Company
First published in Great Britain in 2005 by MQ Publications,
a division of Octopus Publishing Group Ltd
2–4 Heron Quays, London E14 4JP
www.octopusbooks.co.uk

ISBN: 978-184072-967-2

10 9 8 7 6 5 4 3 2

Printed in China

This book contains the opinions and ideas of the author. It is
intended to provide helpful and informative material on the
subjects addressed in this book and is sold with the understanding
that the author and publisher are not engaged in rendering
medical, health, or any other kind of personal professional services
in this book. The reader should consult his or her medical, health,
or competent professional before adopting any of the suggestions
in this book or drawing references from it. The author and
publisher disclaim all responsibility for any liability, loss, or risk,
personal or otherwise, which is incurred as a consequence, directly
or indirectly, of the use and application of any of the contents of
this book.

Safety Note: Those who might be at risk from the effects of
salmonella food poisoning (pregnant and nursing mothers, invalids,
the elderly, young children, and those suffering from immune
deficiency disorders) should consult a medical practitioner with any
concerns about eating raw eggs.

CONTENTS

AcocktailODYSSEY

I can't claim that I become a cocktail aficionado overnight, but I always had a healthy interest in the subject! When I was at college, the cocktails I consumed were generally industrial strength potions and punches...not put together with any great skill, and certainly not downed with any fine appreciation. Names like 'Green Monster' and 'Cement Mixer' were the popular bar calls, generally served in pint glasses and always an effort to finish.

After graduation, time out for adventure seemed like a great idea! I figured that door-to-door selling of aerial photographs in upstate New York might be fun. The reality was disappointing: no joy there, so I set off south to New York City. This was my first encounter with bartenders who were truly passionate about their work and serious about impressing the world with fabulous drinks. As a UK visitor, I didn't have a formal work permit, so finding a job meant working for nothing—literally. Fortunately, bartenders in the U.S. are a class apart. Stateside bartenders hang out with the 'leisure' class—serving and taking care of the social movers and shakers with impressive skill—and that leads to the wonderful and compulsory system of TIPS!

It was amazing! But although I would have loved to stay longer behind Manhattan's bars, I wasn't convinced I was doing the right thing—after all, I was now Allan Gage BSc (Hons), so shouldn't I be wearing a suit and tie? I gave the 9-5 routine a year in London...and loathed every minute of it. How to escape? Well, Mr H and I sold the car and flew to the other side of the world, to the land of opportunity, surfing, and sun: Australia.

From Sydney to Byron Bay, Brisbane to Cairns and many towns between, I spent a couple of years learning about cocktails from some of the finest characters in the business: Jack & Charles at Nick's with their truly upstanding and honorable approach towards the fairer sex; Nina & Murray at Murray's in Brisbane who've been mixing it for 20 years, (love you both!); and Tobin, Joey, and Ed, that bunch of loons at the Establishment—all totally wild!

I learned that there are three types of bartender: showmen—experts at flairing, a hybrid of making drinks and circus skills; mixologists—who have encyclopedic knowledge of drinks and cocktails; and personalities, who focus on their guest's enjoyment. The bartender who unifies elements of all of these is the true Mix Master. I watched, worked with, and played with the best Oz had to offer—and was totally inspired, falling head over heels with the sheer excitement and romance of cocktails.

Bringing my new-found love back to England, I began managing bars in London, wrote a couple of cocktail books to share my new creations; and found myself continually being asked to organize cocktail bars in peoples' homes, parties, weddings, Christmas festivities, birthdays—you name it. "There's an idea here" I thought, "why not recreate that perfect cocktail bar vibe in a one-off situation, in themed environments?"

That's how my company Sweet&Chilli was born! We now produce bars at events of all kinds anywhere in the world. Now, as I make plans to open my idea of the perfect bar, I have visions of beautiful South American waitresses feeding seedless grapes and freshly shucked oysters to a gathering of relaxed and eclectic folk…Martinis and Mojitos mixed with skill and good humor behind a granite bar overlooking the talcum sand of a sun-soaked bay, a smoldering volcano punctuating the horizon, all to a Rolling Stones soundtrack. Sheer heaven!

Meanwhile, here, in the pages of *Cocktail Aficionado* I'm delighted to share my insider knowledge with you! Just go ahead, follow the instructions, and enjoy making delicious cocktails created in the true aficionado's spirit of taste and enjoyment.

Cheers!

 AG

BARnecessities

As I'm a working bartender, serving hundreds of drinks a night, I have to rely upon a whole battery of tools and equipment so that I can deliver any cocktail a customer orders. Fortunately, you won't need as much kit as me—but the following items are easy to get, easy to use, and will help you to make every cocktail in this book as brilliantly as any professional. You'll be the ultimate cocktail aficionado!

Cocktail shaker

The Shaker…every bartender's Excalibur – very few cocktails are possible without one of these so look after it, nurture it and take pride in it. There are several types of cocktail shaker to choose from. The standard model usually comes in gleaming chrome (but may also be made from toughened plastic.) The base, also known as the "can," looks like a tall, cone-shaped tumbler. It has a tight fitting funnel top with built-in strainer holes on which the cap fits snugly. This shaker is best to use at home because it is so straightforward. Why not personalize yours with an engraving…I have 'All Shook Up' on mine.

Mixing (or Boston) glass

A straight, plain glass pitcher used for two purposes. If a cocktail method specifies that a cocktail should be stirred (e.g. Martini, Manhattan,) a Boston glass is used—ingredients poured in, ice added, then stirred using the flat end of a bar spoon. It is also used as the other half of a shaking tin. The two halves are locked together, you shake your cocktail until chilled, then a Hawthorne strainer is used to strain the cocktail into the glass.

Hawthorne Strainer

Place over the shaker can to strain your magical concoction into the relevant glass. Always wash it up straight after use!

Mini Sieve

If you're making a delicious Martini style cocktail, you want to ensure there are no little pieces of ice or fresh fruit in the drink. You want it to be as smooth as possible—so pour the cocktail from the shaker, through the Hawthorne and through the sieve, into your chilled martini glass.

Citrus juicer

Apart from the principle spirit in a cocktail, fruit juice is often the most prevalent ingredient. A step in the right direction to professional expertise is to squeeze your own juices: yes, I said squeeze your own juices. I cannot stress enough how important it is to not go cutting corners. Cocktail aficionados do not cut corners—we do it with perfection in mind and work out the quickest way of achieving it. Electric spinning juicers are ideal for making big batches, but be careful not to overdo it and grind the pith as well; this makes the juice, and therefore the drink, bitter. A simple stainless steel or glass lemon squeezer is fine for small quantities. A cunning little hint is to roll the fruit first on your chopping board with the palm of your hand, applying gentle pressure. When you cut the fruit in half the juice will be released more easily. Although juice extraction seems tedious, the wonderful flavor in the cocktail makes it all worthwhile. Bottled or canned juices can be too sweet or contain preservatives that taint the flavor. If fresh juice makes the drink too sharp, add a little sugar syrup to balance, and that's the key to using citrus juice…balance.

Bar spoon

Also referred to as my magic wand, the classic bar spoon has a long spiral handle with a flat end and an oval or teardrop shaped bowl. It can be used as a measure for delicate measurements, as well as for stirring in a mixing glass, stirring built drinks and muddling ingredients. Also, an advanced use of my beloved bar spoon is for layering shots using the flat-end. Liquids are run down the spiral stem with the spoon inverted into a shot glass.

Muddler

This is a short, rounded, wooden "baton," similar to a pestle. It is used to "mash" or muddle ingredients to release their flavors, often as the first stage in the preparation of a cocktail. Ingredients usually requiring muddling are lime, sugar, mint, vanilla, berries… nowadays you'll see people muddling any number of ingredients. I saw a quail's egg under the muddle once! If you haven't got a muddler *per se,* try a rolling pin, the flat end of a bar spoon, a candle, a marker pen, a wine bottle—improvise!

Jigger

A standard measure for spirits and liqueurs is known as a "jigger," available in many different sizes depending where in the world you are—in Europe millilitres are used, in the U.S. it's fluid ounces. Free-pouring is far more fun and looks so much more impressive though, so take the time to practice and get your pouring accurate—it's well worth it if you're looking to impress your guests.

Chopping board and fruit knife

Make the board wooden and the knife sharp, they're essential for producing impressive looking garnishes.

Blender/Liquidizer

Most domestic blenders will not be able to cope with cubed ice, so always crush your ice before blending a cocktail; having a smooth, sorbet-like quality to your frozen drinks is essential. Make sure it's got a heavy-duty glass, plastic, or stainless steel container and detachable blades to enable thorough cleaning. (Use a bottlebrush for safety and speed when cleaning the blades.) When using the blender to make cocktails, measure in the ingredients, then add crushed ice and start the machine on slow speed, building up speed to produce a smooth, even consistency. No need to strain these blended cocktails, just pour directly into a glass serve with straws.

Ice bucket

The better the ice bucket is insulated, the longer the cubed ice will last. Keep the lid on and use a good pair of tongs to lift the ice out.

Canelle knife

A small tool with a grooved attachment on top used to cut citrus spirals. Hold this against the fruit and steadily drag it round the fruit to get a spiral of peel, thicker and more robust than when using a zester. This is how to produce the famous twist often served in a Martini instead of an olive. Shaken or stirred Sir?

Cocktail sticks

Small wooden or plastic sticks of varying colors, plain or with decorative ends, are used to spear maraschino cherries, olives, small onions, or slices of fruit for garnishing cocktails. Don't re-use cocktail sticks, they are very inexpensive and we are dealing in luxury here!

Citrus zester

I've had mine for years! It's a small metal tool with a line of five small rings on the top set at an angle. It's quite sharp, so you need to hold it firmly against the skin of the citrus fruit and drag it downward, or toward you, to form fine lines of zest. Often used as an attractive garnish on blended cocktails or shaken in to give a light citrus nuance, rather then the intense flavor that comes with fresh citrus juice.

SERVINGglasses

There's no point of going to all the trouble of making great cocktails if you serve them in any old glassware. Always take pride in your drinks and serve them properly, like the true cocktail aficionado you are.

Brandy snifter

Short stemmed with a large balloon-like bowl, it is traditionally used for brandy and some liqueurs. The bulbous cup is designed to let the hand warm the drink while the cup shape wafts the tantalizing aroma to your nose. Though the glass is large in volume, only pour in a small measure of liqueur at a time.

Champagne flute

This tall, elegant glass is an excellent way to serve Champagne, as it both showcases the wine's bouquet while retaining the effervescence for longer due to its small surface area.

Old-fashioned glass

Also known as tumbler, lowball, whiskey, or rocks glass. Short, broad, flat-bottomed glass, essential for serving any drink "on the rocks" (with ice.) Aficionados use this glass for dark spirits with or without mixers and for white spirits, straight.

Highball glass

A clear, simple, tall glass used generally for white spirits and mixer, such as gin and tonic or a Cape Codder (Vodka, Cranberry and lime.)

Collins glass

Taller and thinner than the highball, the Collins glass is often frosted or pebbled with a smooth rim. The Collins glass sometimes has a small stem, known as a Catalina glass. These are absolutely perfect for tall, luxurious and often tropical cocktails.

Boston glass

Tall, chunky, slightly conical glass, also used by pros as a mixing glass.

Cocktail glass

Classic, stemmed glass, often referred to as a "Martini" glass. Used for serving drinks "straight up" (without ice,) the slender stem of the cocktail glass prevents the heat of your hand from warming the contents as you sip. Very elegant in appearance, and any drink served in one of these glasses should be prepared with utmost care.

Margarita glass

Larger and rounder than the traditional cocktail glass, the Margarita has a unique double bowl. Used for Margaritas and Daiquiris, often known as a Coupette.

Champagne saucer

Commonly used for serving Champagne, but drink up swiftly as this elegant glass allows the bubbles and bouquet of the drink to escape faster than the champagne flute.

Goblet

Short, bowl-shaped glass with foot and short stem. A very old-fashioned style, great for aperitifs.

Toddy glass

Short heatproof glass with a small handle, used to serve toddies made of liquor, hot water, and spices. Also used for serving the delicious Irish Coffee cocktail.

Wine goblet

The white wineglass is slightly smaller than the red wineglass, which has a rounder, more balloon-like shape, allowing the subtle complexities of many red wines to be recognized.

Shot glass

A small glass used for serving short drinks with a high alcohol content called "shooters".

BARTENDER'S secrets

I've spent countless happy hours making cocktails (and have the smile lines to prove it) but I'm always curious about knowing more. I can't resist experimenting and aiming for perfection. But, I couldn't do all that without relying on fail-safe techniques— tricks of the trade, if you must. Learn them quickly—they're a fast track to consummate expertise.

Sugar Syrup or Gomme

The most important element in hundreds of cocktails is a balance between sweet and sour. Freshly juiced lemons or limes are the most common sour element, and as we all know, sugar is sweet. However, granulated sugar doesn't dissolve easily in cold drinks, so it is preferable to use "simple syrup" or "sirop de gomme." Gomme can be bought ready made and comes in a variety of flavours (including almond, coconut, vanilla), or it can be homemade. Try this recipe, using a Boston glass as a measure: add 1 measure of boiling water to 1½ measures of caster sugar. Stir until all of the sugar is dissolved and you are left with syrup. Chill this in a sealed container, it will last for about 6 days if kept refrigerated. Try your own infusions—lemongrass, ginger and cinnamon all make delicious syrups.

Creamy cocktails

Always use heavy cream to give the cocktail enough body. Be aware that the action of acid from fruit juices can react with the cream and it may curdle if it is left to stand. So serve the cocktail as soon as it has been made. Always keep the cream refrigerated and wash equipment thoroughly after making cream cocktails, as any remnants will taint your next delicious concoction.

Layering pousse-café

The pousse-café is a multi-colored layered drink, served in a shot glass. Each ingredient is carefully poured into the glass, either down a bar spoon, with the flat end in contact with the surface of the previous ingredient, letting it flow slowly over the top, or over a spoon in contact with the side of the glass and the surface of the drink. Ingredients must be layered according to their alcoholic density. Start with the non-alcoholic ingredients—such as syrups, which are heavy and will stay at the bottom—then work up to the strongest, lightest liquids. The exception is cream and cream liqueurs, which will sit naturally on top of the drink.

Flaming drinks

Care must be taken when igniting drinks. Make sure that there is plenty of space around the glass and that you don't knock it over accidentally. Never carry a drink that is alight.

Extinguish the flames by covering the glass gently with a metal tray. Warn the drinker that the rim will be hot, and let it sit a while so that lips are not burned! To light a drink, the top layer should be a spirit with at least 40% alcohol.

Shake it well

Always remember that cubed ice will both chill and dilute a drink. Surprisingly, the more ice you use, the less the drink will be diluted. (Using too little ice will dilute a drink faster than using more since the smaller quantity melts more rapidly.) For best results, fill the cocktail shaker two-thirds full with fresh ice, then add all ingredients. Attach the top and cap firmly and, holding the shaker in front of you with one hand firmly clasping the top and the other hand supporting the base, shake the cocktail using a brisk pumping action. Do not shake for longer than about five seconds, hard and fast. And remember, never shake fizzy ingredients, the results are explosive!

Stirring

Stirring is best done in a Boston glass. Place cubed ice in the glass, add the ingredients, then stir the drink with a the flat end of your magic bar spoon (try stirring with the oval end — you'll see why,) twirling it gently between thumb and forefinger. When stirring fizzy liquids (especially Champagne) the drink will hold its effervescence longer if stirred gently for just a brief time—but don't be too energetic in the stirring! When the glass shows condensation on the outside, the drink is chilled and ready for pouring.

Frosting rims

Cocktail aficionados rely upon great presentation. For added effect, decorate the top of the glass with salt, sugar, chocolate, or even desiccated coconut. The salt frosting on the rim of a margarita glass is achieved by taking a wedge of lime or lemon and running it around the outside rim of the glass while holding the glass upside down to prevent juice going into the glass or down the stem. Next, dip the outer edge of the glass gently into a saucer of salt until evenly coated. For sugary frostings, dip the rim of the glass into the whipped white of an egg or a wet sponge, then into a saucer of sugar. It is important to only coat the outer edge of the glass, as any coating on the inner rim will taint the liquid.

Chilling glasses

Glasses can be chilled in the fridge, if you have room, or more rapidly in the freezer. To speed chill a warm glass, fill the cocktail glass with ice and soda water before use. (Cracked or crushed ice is better for quicker, more even chilling.) It may take a few minutes for the condensation to appear on the glass to show that it is chilled, but this gives you time to prepare and mix the remaining ingredients.

Using ice

I am a complete ice fanatic! Ideally, buy bags of purified ice cubes, or, if you are making them at home, use bottled mineral or spring water, which tastes purer, and stays clearer when frozen. Do not scrimp or save with ice, a couple of cubes will not do—fill the glass before pouring any liquid in to keep the drink really cold, it just tastes *so* much better. Crushed ice is used extravagantly in many contemporary as well as classic cocktails. Mojitos, Juleps, Daiquiris, all make use of that easy but effective bartending trick—quick chilling and necessary dilution simply by crushing ice cubes—sheer genius! Ideally, to crush ice you should use an electric crusher. Otherwise, use a blender, a manual crusher, or wrap a bag of ice in a tea towel and bash it with a rolling pin.

Infusions

Any spirit with an alcohol content of 40% or more can be flavored with fruit or spices to give an extra dimension to cocktails—but it can't be done in a hurry. One exception is chili-flavored vodka. Just add a few slices of fresh chili to a bottle of vodka, shake the bottle once a day and after 3 days you will have a fiery new brand. Vodka is an ideal base to infuse. Try lemon rind, raspberries, vanilla, basil, lemongrass—anything you want.

Weights and Measurements

These recipes are based on the measurements for one drink. However, ingredients are given in ratio form to make it easy to mix a greater number of cocktails. For one drink, one "measure" corresponds to 1 fl oz US or 25 ml. You can use whatever type of measure you like; a pony holds 1 fl oz U.S., a jigger 1½ fl oz U.S.

Liquid ingredients:

bar spoon	⅟₁₆ fl oz	2 ml
dash	⅛ fl oz	5–10 ml
½ measure	½ fl oz	12.5 ml
1 measure	1fl oz	25 ml
1½ measures	1½ fl oz	37.5 ml
2 measures	2 fl oz	50 ml

vodka

cocktails

Vodka enables you, the aficionado-in-training, to make the most wonderful cocktails; however it has taken quite a long time to gain popularity in the West—it was not until the 1960s and 70s that it became widely fashionable. Nowadays, its versatility and mixability as a cocktail base has made the drink a firm favorite in bars all over the world. Vodka originated in Eastern Europe and was first documented in Russia at the end of the 9th century. Its name comes from the Russian word "Zhizzenia voda," which means water of life (the word "vodka" means "little water"). The spirit is filtered through charcoal to remove impurities, and the result is a pure, clear liquor that gives you the perfect base for a cocktail. It has the kick of alcohol without any heavy taste.

kiwiCAIPIROSKA

- ½ lime, segmented
- ½ skinned kiwi
- 2 teaspoons brown sugar
- sugar syrup to taste
- 2 measures vodka

Muddle the fruit and sugar in the base of a Rocks glass. Add crushed ice and vodka, then sugar syrup to taste. Serve with a stirrer and short straws.

screwDRIVER

- 2 measures vodka
- freshly squeezed orange juice, to top
- orange slices, to garnish

Pour the vodka into an ice-filled highball glass. Top with freshly squeezed orange juice and stir. Garnish with orange slices and serve with straws.

cranKiss

- 1 measure Finlandia Cranberry (cranberry-flavored vodka)
- 1 dash freshly squeezed lime juice
- 1 dash cranberry cordial
- Champagne, to top
- 1 lime twist and cranberries, to garnish

Build all of the ingredients in a Champagne flute, stir, and garnish with the lime twist and cranberries.

CHI-chi

- 1½ measures vodka
- 2 measures pineapple juice
- 1 measure coconut cream
- 1 dash freshly squeezed lime juice
- 1 pineapple slice and 1 cocktail cherry, to garnish

Blend the vodka, pineapple juice, coconut cream, and lime juice with a scoop of crushed ice in a blender. Pour into a coupette or large champagne saucer and garnish with slice of pineapple and cherry.

victoryCOLLINS

- 1½ measures Stolichnaya Vanil
  (vanilla-flavored vodka)
- ½ measure freshly squeezed lemon juice
- 1 bar spoon fine white sugar
- 2 measures grape juice
- orange slices, to garnish

Fill a large highball glass with crushed ice. Shake the vodka, lemon juice, and sugar together (to dissolve) without ice. Pour this mixture over the crushed ice, add the grape juice, and stir. Garnish with slices of orange and serve with straws.

CIELO

- 1½ measures vodka
- 1 measure crème de cassis (black currant liqueur)
- 2 dashes Peychaud's bitters (anise-flavored bitter)
- ½ lime, juice only
- ginger ale, to top
- 1 lime wedge, to garnish

Build all ingredients over ice in a highball glass, stir, and top with ginger ale. Garnish with a wedge of lime and serve with straws.

ignorance

- 1 measure Ketel One Citroen (lemon-flavored vodka)
- ½ measure Campari
- ½ measure passion fruit syrup
- 2 measures apple juice
- 1 orange twist, to garnish

Shake all the ingredients with ice and strain over ice into a large old-fashioned glass, or serve straight up, strained into a chilled martini glass. Garnish with an orange twist.

BLACKrussian

- 1½ measures vodka
- 1 measure Kahlua (coffee liqueur)
- Coca-Cola (optional)

Pour all of the ingredients over ice in an old-fashioned glass (use a highball, if using Coca-Cola) and stir.

cape CODDER

- 2 measures vodka
- 4 measures cranberry juice
- 2 wedges of lime

Pour the vodka and cranberry juice into a highball glass over ice. Squeeze the lime wedges into the drink and drop in. Stir, and serve with straws.

elderflower FIZZ

- 1 measure Polstar Cucumber (cucumber-flavored vodka)
- ½ measure elderflower cordial
- Champagne, to top
- lemon peel
- 2 peeled cucumber slices

Pour all of the ingredients into a Champagne saucer. Wipe the rim of the glass with the lemon peel, stir, and garnish with the two slices of skinless cucumber.

BLOODY mary (ORIGINAL)

- 2 measures vodka
- 6 measures tomato juice
- 1 dash freshly squeezed lemon juice
- 4 dashes Worcestershire sauce
- ½ teaspoon cayenne pepper
- salt and pepper, to taste
- 1 lime wedge, to garnish

Shake all of the ingredients (except the lime wedge) with ice and strain into a highball glass over ice. Add the wedge of lime and serve with a straw.

BLOODY caesar

- 2 measures vodka
- 4 dashes Worcestershire sauce
- 2 dashes Tabasco sauce
- 6 measures clamato juice
- 1 teaspoon horseradish
- celery salt and freshly ground black pepper, to taste
- 1 stick of celery, to garnish

Mix all of the ingredients in a shaker, add ice, and shake briefly to mix. Strain the mix into a highball glass over ice and garnish with a stick of celery.

plasma

- ½ teaspoon Dijon mustard
- 1 teaspoon fresh dill, chopped
- 2 measures Wyborowa Pepper (pepper-flavored vodka)
- 2 drops Tabasco sauce
- 4 drops Worcestershire sauce
- ½ lemon, juice only
- celery salt and freshly ground black pepper, to taste
- 4 measures tomato juice
- 2 6-inch strips of cucumber and $^1/_2$ cherry tomato
- seasoned with salt and pepper, to garnish

Muddle the mustard and dill together in the base of a shaker to form a paste, then add all of the other ingredients with some ice. Shake to mix then strain into a highball glass over ice. Garnish with strips of cucumber and half a seasoned cherry tomato.

COSMOPOLITAN

- 1½ measures Ketel One Citroen (lemon-flavored vodka)
- 1 measure triple sec
- 1 dash freshly squeezed lime juice
- 1 measure cranberry juice
- 1 flamed orange twist, to garnish

Shake all of the liquid ingredients with ice and strain into a chilled martini glass. Flame the orange twist over the surface as follows: cut a small oval of peel from an orange, leaving a little pith intact. Pinch the oval skin-side out holding it over a flame. Squeeze it firmly so that the zest oil is released. The zest oil will then ignite to give you an impressive flame, with a fantastic aroma. Drop the twist into the drink.

mandrapolitan

- 1½ measures Absolut Mandrin (orange-flavored vodka)
- 1 measure Cointreau
- 1 measure cranberry juice
- 1 dash freshly squeezed lime juice
- 4 drops orange bitters
- 1 lime twist, to garnish

Shake all of the ingredients with ice and strain into a chilled martini glass. Garnish with a lime twist.

SEAbreeze

- 2 measures vodka
- 4 measures cranberry juice
- 2 measures freshly squeezed grapefruit juice
- lime wedges, to garnish

Build all of the ingredients over ice in a highball glass, stir, and garnish with lime wedges. Serve with straws.

bayBREEZE

- 2 measures vodka
- 4 measures cranberry juice
- 2 measures pineapple juice
- lime wedges, to garnish

Fill a highball glass with ice, then add the vodka, cranberry, and pineapple juice. Stir and garnish with wedges of lime.

VODKAmartini

- ½ measure dry vermouth
- 2 measures chilled vodka
- 2 green pitted olives, to garnish

Fill a mixing glass with ice and add the vermouth. Stir the contents to coat the ice and pour off any liquid, leaving only the flavored ice. Add the vodka and stir to chill. Double strain the mix into a chilled martini glass and garnish with two olives on a cocktail stick.

saketini

- 1 measure vodka
- 1½ measures sake
- ½ measure orange curaçao
- 4 drops orange bitters
- 2 peeled cucumber slices, to garnish

Add all of the liquid ingredients to a mixing glass and add ice. Stir until thoroughly chilled and double strain into a chilled martini glass. Garnish with two thin slices of peeled cucumber. NB This is also delicious by simply substituting gin for the vodka.

FRENCHmartini

- 2 measures vodka
- ½ measure Chambord (French black raspberry liqueur)
- 1 measure pineapple juice
- 1 plump raspberry, to garnish

Pour all of the liquid ingredients into a shaker and add ice. Shake vigorously and strain into a chilled martini glass. Allow to settle briefly, then float the raspberry in the center of the surface foam.

vesper

- 1½ measures vodka
- 1½ measures gin
- ½ measure dry vermouth
- 1 lemon twist, to garnish

Shake all of the ingredients with ice and double strain into a chilled martini glass. Garnish with a twist of lemon.

POLISHmartini

- 1 measure Wyborowa Vodka (Polish vodka)
- 1 measure Zubrowka Bison Grass Vodka

Stir all ingredients with ice to chill thoroughly and double strain into a chilled martini glass. Garnish with a twist of lemon.

gardenMARTINI

- 1 measure krupnik vodka (honey-flavored vodka)
- 1 measure freshly pressed apple juice
- 1 lemon twist, to garnish

Stir all ingredients with ice to chill thoroughly and double strain into a chilled martini glass. Garnish with a twist of lemon.

TARTEtatinMARTINI

- 1½ measures Stolichnaya Vanil (vanilla-flavored vodka)
- 1 dash orgeat syrup (almond syrup)
- ½ measure apple schnapps
- 1 dash lemonade
- whipped cream, to float
- ground cinnamon, for dusting

Stir the vodka, syrup, and schnapps with ice to chill and strain into a chilled martini glass. Add the dash of lemonade and then float the cream on the surface. Dust the surface with ground cinnamon.

metrotini

- 4 blueberries
- 6 raspberries
- 2 measures krupnik vodka (honey-flavored vodka)
- ½ measure Chambord (French black raspberry liqueur)
- 1 measure freshly squeezed lemon juice

Muddle the blueberries, plus four of the raspberries (reserving two for a garnish) in the base of a shaker, add the liquid ingredients, and shake with ice. Strain into a chilled martini glass and garnish with the remaining two raspberries on a swizzle stick.

mitchMARTINI

- 1½ measures Zubrowka Bison Grass Vodka
- ½ measure passion fruit syrup
- ½ measure peach liqueur
- 1 measure freshly pressed apple juice
- 1 lemon twist, to garnish

Shake all of the liquid ingredients with ice and double strain into a chilled martini glass. Garnish with a lemon twist.

MARTINIroyale

- 2 measures frozen vodka
- 1 dash crème de cassis (black currant liqueur)
- Champagne, to top
- 1 lemon twist, to garnish

Pour the vodka and cassis into a frozen martini glass and gently stir. Top with chilled Champagne and garnish with a twist of lemon.

zelda**MARTINI**

- 5 mint leaves
- 1 dash orgeat syrup (almond syrup)
- 2 measures Zubrowka Bison Grass Vodka
- ½ measure chilled water
- 1 measure freshly squeezed lime juice
- 1 mint sprig, to garnish

Bruise the mint leaves with the orgeat syrup in the base of a shaker. Add the vodka, water, and lime, then shake with ice. Double strain the mix into a chilled martini glass and garnish with the mint sprig.

watermelon**MARTINI**

- 4 chunks fresh watermelon
- 1 dash freshly squeezed lime juice
- 1 dash sugar syrup
- 2 measures Wyborowa Melon (melon-flavored vodka)
- ½ measure Passoã (passion fruit liqueur)
- 1 wedge of fresh watermelon, to garnish

In the base of a shaker, muddle the watermelon flesh, lime juice, and sugar syrup. Then add the vodka and Passoã. Fill with ice and shake vigorously. Double strain into a chilled martini glass and garnish with a lime twist.

twinkle

- 3 measures vodka
- ½ measure elderflower cordial
- Champagne, to top
- 1 lemon twist, to garnish

Shake the vodka and elderflower cordial together and double strain into a large, chilled martini glass. Top with chilled Champagne, stir, and garnish with a lemon twist.

ESPRESSOmartini

- 1½ measures vodka
- 1 measure cold espresso
- ½ measure Kahlua (coffee liqueur)
- 1 dash sugar syrup

Shake all ingredients together with ice and strain into a chilled martini glass.

vanillaHAZE

- 2 measures Stolichnaya Vanil (vanilla-flavored vodka)
- ½ measure passion fruit juice
- ½ measure passion fruit syrup
- 2 drops orange bitters
- 1 measure freshly pressed apple juice
- 4 mint leaves
- 1 mint sprig, to garnish

Shake all of the ingredients with ice and double strain into a chilled martini glass. Garnish with the mint sprig.

VOCHACINO

- 1 measure vodka
- ½ measure Kahlua (coffee liqueur)
- ½ measure sugar syrup
- ½ measure cold espresso
- ½ teaspoon cocoa powder, plus a
    little extra for dusting
- 1 measure light cream

Shake all of the ingredients vigorously with ice and strain into a chilled martini glass. Garnish the surface by dusting with cocoa powder.

APPLEsip

- 2 measures Stolichnaya Vanil (vanilla-flavored vodka)
- 1 measure apple brandy
- 1 dash cinnamon syrup
- 1 measure freshly pressed apple juice
- 2 slices peeled apple, to garnish

Shake all of the liquid ingredients with ice and double strain into a chilled martini glass. Garnish with slices of peeled apple.

roadRUNNER

- 1½ measures vodka
- 1 measure amaretto
- ½ measure coconut cream
- 1 measure heavy cream
- ground nutmeg, for dusting

Shake all of the ingredients with ice and strain into a chilled martini glass. Dust the surface of the drink with ground nutmeg.

from RUSSIA with LOVE

- 5 mint leaves
- 5 basil leaves
- 1 teaspoon sugar syrup
- 3 measures Stolichnaya Strasberi (strawberry-flavored vodka)
- 1 basil leaf and 1 split strawberry, to garnish

In the base of a shaker, bruise the mint and basil with the sugar syrup using a muddler. Add the vodka, fill with ice, and stir until chilled. Double strain the mix into a chilled martini glass and garnish with the split strawberry and basil leaf.

AVALON

- 1½ measures vodka
- ½ measure Pisang Ambon (Dutch banana-based liqueur)
- 2 measures freshly pressed apple juice
- 1 dash freshly squeezed lemon juice
- lemonade, to top
- red apple slices, to garnish

Fill a highball glass with ice. Build the vodka, Pisang Ambon, and apple and lemon juice in the glass. Stir and top with lemonade. Garnish with slices of red apple.

APPLEblossom

- 1 measure vodka
- 1 measure apple brandy
- 2 measures freshly pressed apple juice
- 1 dash freshly squeezed lemon juice
- 1 lemon twist, to garnish

Stir all of the ingredients with ice in a mixing glass. Strain over ice into an old-fashioned glass. Garnish with a lemon twist.

holyWATER

- 1½ measures vodka
- ½ measure triple sec
- ½ measure light rum
- tonic water, to top
- 1 dash of grenadine
- 1 lemon, rind only, to garnish

Build the vodka, triple sec, and rum over ice in a large highball glass, stir, and charge with tonic water. Drizzle the grenadine through the drink before serving and garnish with the rind from a whole lemon.

MOSCOWmule

- 2 measures vodka
- ½ lime, cut into wedges
- ginger ale, to top

Add the vodka to an ice-filled highball glass, squeeze the lime wedges into the glass (drop into the drink once squeezed), stir, and top with ginger ale. Serve with straws.

Long**BEACHiced**TEA

- ½ measure vodka
- ½ measure gin
- ½ measure light rum
- ½ measure tequila
- ½ measure triple sec
- 1 dash freshly squeezed lime juice
- cranberry juice, to top
- lime wedges, to garnish

Add all of the alcoholic ingredients and lime juice to a shaker, add ice, and shake briefly. Strain into an ice-filled highball glass and top with cranberry juice. Stir, garnish with lime wedges, and serve with straws.

LOU'sicedTEA

- 2 measures Absolut Citron (lemon-flavored vodka)
- 1 measure cranberry juice
- ½ measure freshly squeezed orange juice
- 4 measures chilled Earl Grey tea
- 1 dash freshly squeezed lemon juice
- 4 mint leaves
- 1 dash sugar syrup
- lemon slices, to garnish

Shake all ingredients with ice and strain into a large ice-filled highball glass. Garnish with lemon slices and serve with straws.

BLOSSOM

- ½ lime, juice only
- 2 measures Absolut Kurant (berry-flavored vodka)
- ½ measure cold water
- 1 dash lime cordial
- 1 lime twist, to garnish

Squeeze the lime into a shaker, then add the other ingredients. Shake with ice and double strain into a chilled martini glass. Garnish with a lime twist.

bison'sPLUMS

- 2 measures Zubrowka Bison Grass Vodka
- 2 measures freshly pressed apple juice
- 1 measure Mirabelle plum purée
- 1 dash freshly squeezed lemon juice
- lemon slices, to garnish

Shake all of the ingredients together and strain over ice into a slim highball glass. Garnish with lemon slices and serve with straws.

HARVEYwallbanger

- 2 measures vodka
- 4 measures freshly squeezed orange juice
- ½ measure Galliano
- 1 orange slice, to garnish

Pour the vodka and orange juice into a large ice-filled highball glass and stir. Float some Galliano on top, garnish with an orange slice and serve with straws.

RUSSIAN spring PUNCH

- 1 measure Stolichnaya Vodka (Russian vodka)
- 1 measure freshly squeezed lemon juice
- ½ measure raspberry purée
- ½ measure créme de cassis (black currant liqueur)
- 1 dash framboise (raspberry liqueur)
- 1 dash sugar syrup
- champagne, to top
- 2 lemon slices and raspberries, to garnish

Shake all ingredients except champagne with ice and strain over crushed ice into a sling glass. Top with champagne, stir, and garnish with two lemon slices and fresh raspberries.

rapaska

- 2 measures Stolichnaya Razberi (raspberry-flavored vodka)
- 1 measure passion fruit purée
- 1 measure raspberry purée
- ½ passion fruit
- 1 measure freshly pressed apple juice
- 1 measure freshly squeezed orange juice
- 2 raspberries and 1 apple wedge, to garnish

Shake all of the ingredients briefly with crushed ice and transfer to a highball glass. Do not strain. Garnish with raspberries and an apple wedge, and serve with straws.

KINKYmole

- 2 measures Absolut Kurant (berry-flavored vodka)
- 1 dash orgeat syrup (almond syrup)
- 2 measures freshly squeezed pink grapefruit juice
- 2 dashes crème de mure (blackberry liqueur)
- 2 blackberries, to garnish

Shake all of the liquid ingredients and strain over ice into a large highball glass. Garnish with blackberries and serve with straws.

honeyBERRYsour

- 1½ measures krupnik vodka (honey-flavored vodka)
- ½ measure Chambord (French black raspberry liqueur)
- 1 measure freshly squeezed lemon juice
- 1 dash sugar syrup
- 2 raspberries, to garnish

Shake all of the liquid ingredients with ice and strain over ice into a large old-fashioned glass. Garnish with two raspberries and serve with straws.

RISINGsun

- 2 measures vodka
- 2 measures freshly squeezed grapefruit juice
- ½ measure passion fruit syrup
- ½ lemon, juice only
- pink grapefruit slice, to garnish

Shake all of the ingredients together and strain over ice in a large old-fashioned glass. Garnish with a slice of pink grapefruit and serve with straws

passionCHARGE

- 1 passion fruit
- 1 dash freshly squeezed lime juice
- 1 dash passion fruit syrup
- 2 measures cranberry juice
- 1½ measures Absolut Mandrin (orange-flavored vodka)
- Red Bull (stimulation drink,) to top
- lime wedges, to garnish

Spoon the flesh of the passion fruit into the base of a highball glass. Add lime juice, syrup, cranberry juice, and vodka. Fill the highball glass with ice, transfer to a shaker, shake, and return to the glass, unstrained. Top with Red Bull, stir, and garnish with lime wedges. Serve with straws.

MISSscarlett

- 8 fresh raspberries
- ½ lime, cut into wedges
- 1 dash sugar syrup
- 2 measures Stolichnaya Razberi
    (raspberry-flavored vodka)
- soda water, to top.

In the base of a highball glass, muddle the raspberries, lime, and sugar syrup. Fill the glass with ice, and add the vodka. Transfer the contents of the glass into a shaker and shake. Then pour back into the highball glass. Do not strain. Top with soda water, stir, and serve with straws.

KUMQUATmay

- 5 kumquats, chopped
- 1 dash cinnamon syrup
- ½ measure kiwi schnapps
- 1½ measures Absolut Vanilla (vanilla-flavored vodka)

Briefly muddle the chopped kumquats with the cinnamon syrup in the base of a shaker. Then add all the other ingredients, shake with ice, and transfer to a large old-fashioned glass, unstrained. Serve with straws.

MADRAS

- 2 measures vodka
- 4 measures cranberry juice
- 2 measures freshly squeezed orange juice
- orange slices, to garnish

Build all of the ingredients over ice in a highball glass, stir, and garnish with orange slices. Serve with straws.

kitschREVOLT

- 1 measure Absolut Kurant (berry-flavored vodka)
- ½ measure strawberry purée
- Champagne, to top
- strawberry slices, to garnish

Shake the vodka and strawberry purée together briefly with ice and strain into a chilled flute. Top with Champagne, stir, and garnish with slices of strawberry.

FRESCA

- 1 small pink grapefruit, segmented
- 1 teaspoon brown sugar
- 2 measures vodka
- lemonade, to top

Muddle the grapefruit and sugar in the base of a boston glass until sugar is dissolved, then fill the glass with ice. Add vodka and stir, then top with lemonade. Stir again and serve with a stirrer and straws.

'57CHEVY

- 1 measure vodka
- 1 measure Southern Comfort
- ½ measure Grand Marnier
- 2 measures pineapple juice
- 1 dash freshly squeezed lemon juice
- pineapple wedges, to garnish

Shake all of the ingredients with ice and strain into a highball glass over ice. Garnish with pineapple wedges.

peterPAN

- 1½ measures vodka
- ½ measure Frangelico (hazelnut liqueur)
- 1 measure Poire William (Pear brandy)

Stir all ingredients with ice in a mixing glass. Double strain into a chilled Martini glass and garnish with a single purple rose petal.

BUCK'Stwizz

- 1 peeled pink grapefruit slice
- 1 measure Absolut Mandrin (orange-flavored vodka)
- 1 measure freshly squeezed orange juice
- ½ measure maraschino liqueur
- Champagne, to top

Place the slice of pink grapefruit in the bottom of a large Champagne saucer. Briefly shake the vodka, orange juice, and liqueur with ice and strain over the grapefruit. Top with Champagne, and stir.

POTshot

- 1 lime wedge
- 1 measure Absolut Kurant (berry-flavored vodka)
- 1 dash peach schnapps

Squeeze the lime wedge into a shaker; add the vodka and schnapps, then shake briefly with ice. Strain into a chilled shot glass, and drink it in one gulp.

SWIZZLE

- 1 dash passion fruit syrup
- 1 dash Campari
- 1 measure Grey Goose L'orange
  (quality orange-flavored vodka)

Layer the ingredients in the following order: syrup, Campari, vodka.

OYSTERshot

- 1 small plump oyster
- 3 drops Tabasco sauce
- 2 drops Worcestershire sauce
- pinch salt
- pinch black pepper
- 1 squeezed lemon wedge
- ½ measure chilled Absolut Peppar
    (pepper-flavored vodka)
- ½ measure tomato juice

In a shot glass, build the ingredients in the exact order detailed above, starting with the oyster. Stir the shot briefly and let it slip
down in one.

BLOODYsimple

- 1 ripe tomato wedge
- celery salt and freshly ground
- black pepper, to taste
- 1 measure chilled Absolut Peppar
    (pepper-flavored vodka)
- 2 drops Tabasco sauce

Season a wedge of ripe tomato with celery salt and pepper. Pour the chilled vodka into a shot glass and add two drops of Tabasco. Serve with the tomato.

RAFF SLAMMER

- 1 measure vodka
- 1 measure bitter lemon

Add all of the ingredients to an old-fashioned glass. Cover the glass with your hand, slam firmly three times against a hard, stable surface, and down the drink in one while it is still fizzing.

383

- ¼ measure Frangelico
- 1 measure chilled Stolichnaya Razberi (raspberry-flavored vodka)
- orange wedge dusted with brown
- sugar, to garnish

Pour the Frangelico and then the chilled vodka into a shot glass. Down this in one mouthful and follow it with a bite of the sugared orange.

kamikaze

- 1 measure vodka
- ½ measure Cointreau
- 2 dashes freshly squeezed lemon juice

Shake all of the ingredients very briefly with ice and strain into a shot glass. This shot is best made in larger quantities, so either share some or have a few. Add a dash of Chambord before drinking and this becomes a Purple Haze.

BODYshot

- 1 teaspoon white sugar
- 1 measure chilled vodka
- 1 lemon wedge

Lick your partner's neck to moisten. Pour the sugar onto his/her neck in the moistened area. Place wedge of lemon in his/her mouth with the skin pointed inward. You must first lick the sugar from his/her neck, then the vodka, then suck the lemon from their mouth. What an ice-breaker!

PINKsin

- 1 teaspoon fine white sugar
- 1 dash red food coloring
- 1 measure chilled Absolut Mandrin
    (orange-flavored vodka)
- 1 dash framboise (raspberry liqueur)
- 1 lime wedge coated, to garnish

Mix a spoonful of fine white sugar with a drop of red food coloring, to create pink sugar and use it to coat the lime wedge. Add the chilled vodka and liqueur to a shot glass, stirring to mix. Serve with the lime wedge coated in pink sugar.

2

cocktails

If you want to win a glittering reputation as a serious cocktail aficionado-mixologist, you'll need to become acquainted with the marvellous qualities of that legendary elixir called gin. After all, it's the foundation of the martini—the classic cocktail. It was in the cocktail-mad 1920s that gin began to be drunk by high society, most commonly enjoyed with tonic and a wedge of lime, or in a martini. Originally used for medicinal purposes, gin was first produced in Holland in the 17th century. It is made by distilling spirit with various herbs and other botanicals—each producer has a characteristic formula that distinguishes the character and quality of the final product. The name "gin" was taken from the French word for juniper, "genievre," as juniper is one of many flavors that is added to the spirit.

MAYFLOWERmartini

- 1½ measures gin
- ½ measure apricot brandy
- 1 measure freshly pressed apple juice
- 1 dash elderflower cordial
- ½ measure freshly squeezed lemon juice
- 1 edible flower petal, to garnish

Shake all of the ingredients with ice and double strain into a chilled martini glass. Float the petal on the drinks surface as a garnish.

PARADISEmartini

- 2 measures gin
- 1½ measures freshly squeezed orange juice
- ½ measure apricot brandy
- 4 drops orange bitters
- 1 flamed orange twist (see page 25)

Shake all of the ingredients with ice and then double strain into a chilled martini glass. Flame the orange twist over the drink's surface and drop it in.

ladyMARTINI

- 1½ measures gin
- ½ measure apple brandy
- ½ measure freshly squeezed lemon juice
- 1 dash orgeat syrup (almond syrup)
- ½ egg white

Shake all of the ingredients with ice and strain into a chilled martini glass.

martini**THYME**

- 1 bunch of lemon thyme, stalks removed
- 1 dash sugar syrup
- 1½ measures gin
- 1 measure Green Chartreuse (herb liqueur)
- 3 olives, to garnish

Reserve a lemon thyme leaf to use as a garnish.
Muddle the rest of the thyme with the sugar syrup in
the base of a shaker. Add remaining ingredients, shake
with ice, and double strain into a chilled martini glass.
Garnish with three olives and the reserved
lemon thyme leaf on a swizzle stick.

BLUEbird

- 3 measures gin
- 1 measure triple sec
- 4 drops Angostura bitters
- 1 lemon twist, to garnish

Shake the first three ingredients with ice and strain
into a chilled martini glass. Garnish with a lemon twist.

AVIATION

- 1½ measures gin
- 2 dashes maraschino cherry liqueur
- 1 measure freshly squeezed lemon juice
- 1 cocktail cherry, to garnish

Shake first three ingredients with ice and strain into a
chilled martini glass. Garnish with a single cocktail cherry.

raspberry**MARTINI**

- 8 raspberries
- 1 dash sugar syrup
- 1 measure sloe gin
- 1 measure gin
- ½ measure framboise (raspberry liqueur)
- 2 raspberries, to garnish

Muddle the raspberries and sugar syrup in the base of a shaker, then add all the other ingredients and shake vigorously with ice. Double strain into a chilled martini glass and float two raspberries on the surface.

breakfas**TMARTINI**

- 1 teaspoon orange marmalade
- 2 measures gin
- 1 dash freshly squeezed lemon juice
- ½ measure triple sec
- 1 small triangle of toast spread
  with butter and marmalade

Stir the marmalade with the gin in a shaker until dissolved, then add the lemon juice and triple sec. Shake until thoroughly chilled. Strain into a chilled martini glass and garnish with the toast slice.

Opa**MARTINI**

- 2 measures gin
- 1 measure triple sec or Cointreau
- 2 measures freshly squeezed orange juice
- 1 flamed orange twist (see page 25)

Shake all of the ingredients with ice and strain into a
chilled martini glass. Garnish with a flamed orange twist.

WIBBLE

- 1 measure sloe gin
- 1 measure gin
- 1 measure freshly squeezed grapefruit juice
- 1 dash freshly squeezed lemon juice
- 1 dash sugar syrup
- 1 dash crème de mure (blackberry liqueur)
- 1 lemon twist

Shake all the ingredients with ice and strain into a
chilled martini glass. Squeeze the oils from the lemon
twist over the drink's surface and drop in as a garnish.

MAIDEN'S**blush**

- 1½ measures gin
- ½ measure triple sec
- 1 dash grenadine
- 1 dash freshly squeezed lemon juice
- lemon slices, to garnish

Shake all of the liquid ingredients with ice and strain
into an ice-filled old-fashioned glass. Garnish with
lemon slices and serve with short straws.

gimlet

- 2 measures gin
- 1 measure lime cordial
- ½ measure water (optional)
- 1 lime wedge

Stir all of the liquid ingredients with ice until thoroughly chilled and strain into a chilled martini glass. Squeeze the lime wedge over the drink and drop in.

invitationONLY

- 3 measures gin
- ½ measure sugar syrup
- ½ measure freshly squeezed lime juice
- 1 egg white
- 1 dash crème de mure (blackberry liqueur)
- 2 blackberries, to garnish

Shake and strain the first four ingredients over ice into a highball glass. Lace the drink with crème de mure and garnish with two blackberries.

MAXIM

- 1½ measures gin
- 1 measure dry vermouth
- 1 dash white crème de cacao
    (chocolate-flavored liqueur)
- 1 cocktail cherry

Shake all of the ingredients with ice until thoroughly chilled, then strain into a chilled martini glass. Garnish with a cocktail cherry.

GIBSONmartini

- ½ measure extra dry vermouth
- 2 measures gin
- 4 pearl onions

Stir the vermouth with ice in a mixing glass then strain away any excess liquid so just the coated ice remains. Add the gin and stir until thoroughly chilled. Strain the mix into a chilled martini glass and garnish with the onions on a swizzle stick. Garnished with an olive or lemon twist instead this will become a Dry Martini (see 55).

paisleyMARTINI

- 1½ measures gin
- ½ measure extra dry vermouth
- 2 dashes Scotch whisky
- 1 lemon twist, to garnish

Shake all of the liquid ingredients with ice and strain into a chilled martini glass. Garnish with a lemon twist.

ALEXANDER'Ssister

- 1½ measures gin
- 1 measure green crème de menthe
- 1 measure light cream
- grated nutmeg, to garnish

Shake all of the liquid ingredients with ice and strain into a chilled martini glass. Finish with a sprinkle of grated nutmeg.

PARKavenue

- 1½ measures gin
- 1 measure sweet vermouth
- 1 dash pineapple juice

Stir all of the ingredients in a mixing glass with ice until thoroughly chilled. Strain into a chilled martini glass and serve immediately.

hedgerowSLING

- 2 measures sloe gin
- 1 measure freshly squeezed lemon juice
- 1 dash sugar syrup
- soda water, to top
- ½ measure crème de mure (blackberry liqueur)
- 3 blueberries, 3 blackberries and
    1 lemon slice, to garnish

Shake the gin, lemon juice, and sugar syrup with ice, and strain into an ice-filled highball glass. Top with soda water and lace with the crème de mure. Garnish with blueberries, blackberries, and a lemon slice.

BRONX

- 2 measures gin
- ½ measure extra dry vermouth
- ½ measure sweet vermouth
- 1½ measures blood orange juice
- 1 cocktail cherry, to garnish

Shake all of the liquid ingredients with ice and strain into an old-fashioned glass over crushed ice. Garnish with a cocktail cherry and serve with short straws.

DRYmartini

- ½ measure Noilly Prat (dry vermouth)
- 2 measures gin
- 1 olive or 1 lemon twist, to garnish

Stir the vermouth with ice in a mixing glass then strain away any excess liquid so that just the coated ice remains. Add the gin and stir until chilled. Strain the mix into a chilled martini glass and garnish with a lemon twist or olive on a cocktail stick.

BRONX

- 2 measures gin
- ½ measure extra dry vermouth
- ½ measure sweet vermouth
- 1½ measures blood orange juice
- 1 cocktail cherry, to garnish

Shake all of the liquid ingredients with ice and strain into an old-fashioned glass over crushed ice. Garnish with a cocktail cherry and serve with short straws.

TOMcollins

- 2 measures gin
- 1 measure freshly squeezed lemon juice
- ½ measure sugar syrup
- soda water, to top
- 1 lemon slice, to garnish

Shake the first three ingredients with ice and strain into an ice-filled highball glass. Top with soda and stir gently. Garnish with a lemon slice and serve with straws.

SLOE-ho

- 1 measure sloe gin
- 1 measure gin
- ½ measure Chambord (black raspberry liqueur)
- 1 dash freshly squeezed lemon juice
- 1 dash sugar syrup
- ½ egg white
- soda water, to top
- 1 lemon twist, to garnish

Shake the first six ingredients with ice and strain into an ice-filled highball glass. Top with soda water. Garnish with a lemon twist and serve with straws.

gingerTOM

- 2 measures gin
- ½ measure ginger syrup
- 1 measure freshly squeezed lime juice
- 1 dash sugar syrup
- sparkling mineral water, to top
- 1 lime wedge and 1 mint sprig, to garnish

Fill a highball glass with ice and add the gin, ginger syrup, lime juice, and sugar syrup. Stir gently to mix, then top with sparkling mineral water. Garnish with a squeeze of lime and a mint sprig.

GREENBACK

- 1½ measures gin
- 1 measure green crème de menthe
- 1 measure freshly squeezed lemon juice
- lemon slices, to garnish

Shake all of the ingredients briefly with ice and strain into an old-fashioned glass over ice. Garnish with lemon slices and serve with short straws.

bramble

- 2 measures gin
- 1½ measures freshly squeezed lemon juice
- ½ measure sugar syrup
- ½ measure crème de mure (blackberry liqueur)
- 1 blackberry and 1 lemon slice, to garnish

Fill an old-fashioned glass with crushed ice, add the first three ingredients, and stir. Top glass with more crushed ice then lace with crème de mure. Garnish with a blackberry and lemon slice and serve with two short straws.

ARTHURtompkins

- 2 measures gin
- ½ measure Grand Marnier
- 1 dash freshly squeezed lemon juice
- 1 lemon twist, to garnish

Shake the gin, Grand Marnier, and lemon juice briefly with ice and strain into an old-fashioned glass over ice. Garnish with a twist of lemon and serve with short straws.

GINsour

- 2 measures gin
- 2 measures freshly squeezed orange juice
- 1 measure freshly squeezed lemon juice
- 1 measure egg white
- ½ measure sugar syrup
- 1 lemon wedge, to garnish

Shake all of the liquid ingredients with ice and strain into an ice-filled highball glass. Garnish with a lemon wedge and serve with straws.

FRENCH75

- 1 measure gin
- ½ measure freshly squeezed lemon juice
- 1 dash sugar syrup
- Champagne, to top
- 1 lemon twist, to garnish

Shake the gin, lemon juice, and sugar syrup with ice and strain into a Champagne flute. Top with the Champagne, stir, and garnish with a lemon twist.

ginGEENIE

- 6 mint leaves
- ½ measure freshly squeezed lemon juice
- 1 dash sugar syrup
- 2 measures gin
- 1 mint sprig, to garnish

Muddle the mint leaves, lemon juice, and sugar syrup in the bottom of an old-fashioned glass. Fill with crushed ice and stir. Slowly add the gin and stir again. Garnish with a sprig of mint and serve with straws.

bumbleBEE

- 1 teaspoon liquid honey
- 1 dash freshly squeezed lemon juice
- 2 measures gin
- 2 lemon slices, to garnish

Fill an old-fashioned glass with crushed ice and add honey and lemon juice. Stir while slowly adding gin and top with more crushed ice. Garnish with lemon slices and serve with short straws.

PALMbeach

- 1 measure gin
- ½ measure extra dry vermouth
- 1 measure grapefruit juice
- 1 dash sugar syrup
- 1 pink grapefruit wedge, to garnish

Shake all of the ingredients with ice and strain into an ice-filled highball glass. Garnish with a pink grapefruit wedge and serve with straws.

SWEETgeenie

- 6 mint leaves
- ½ measure freshly squeezed lemon juice
- 1 dash sugar syrup
- 1½ measures gin
- ½ measure amaretto
- 1 mint sprig, to garnish

Muddle the mint leaves, lemon juice, and sugar syrup in the bottom of an old-fashioned glass. Fill with crushed ice and stir. Slowly add the gin and stir again. Top with amaretto and garnish with a mint sprig. Serve with short straws.

singaporeSLING

- 2 measures gin
- 1 measure freshly squeezed orange juice
- 1 measure freshly squeezed lime juice
- 1 dash lime cordial
- 3 drops Angostura bitters
- 2 dashes Cherry Heering (cherry liqueur)
- soda water, to top
- 1 dash Benedictine (liqueur)
- 1 split lemon slice and 1 cherry, to garnish

Shake the gin, orange juice, lime juice, lime cordial, bitters, and 1 dash of the cherry liqueur with ice and strain into an ice-filled sling glass. Top with soda water and slowly add the remaining cherry liqueur and Benedictine so they float at the top of the glass. Garnish with a split lemon slice and a cherry, and serve with straws.

sloeGINfizz

- 1 measure sloe gin
- 1 measure gin
- 1 measure freshly squeezed lime juice
- 1 dash sugar syrup
- ½ egg white
- soda water, to top
- lemon slices, to garnish

Shake the sloe gin, gin, lime juice, sugar syrup, and egg white with ice, and strain over ice into an old-fashioned glass. Top with soda water, stir, and garnish with slices of lemon.

ORANGEbuck

- 1½ measures gin
- 1 measure freshly squeezed orange juice
- 1 dash freshly squeezed lime juice
- ginger ale, to top
- lime wedges, to garnish

Shake all of the ingredients with ice and strain into an ice-filled highball glass. Top with the ginger ale and stir. Garnish with lime wedges and serve with straws.

negroni

- 1 measure gin
- 1 measure Campari
- 1 measure sweet vermouth
- soda water (optional), to top
- ½ orange slice, to garnish

Stir the gin, Campari, and vermouth in a mixing glass with ice and strain into an ice-filled highball glass. Top with soda and garnish with half an orange slice. Serve with short straws and a stirrer.

RASPBERRYcollins

- 2 measures gin
- 1½ measures raspberry purée
- ½ measure freshly squeezed lemon juice
- ½ measure crème de framboise (raspberry liqueur)
- 1 dash sugar syrup
- 1 dash orange bitters
- soda water, to top
- 2 raspberries and 1 lemon slice, to garnish

Shake first six ingredients with ice and strain into a highball glass filled with crushed ice. Top with soda water and stir. Garnish with raspberries and a lemon slice, serve with straws.

shadyGROVEcooler

- 2 measures gin
- 1 measure freshly squeezed lime juice
- ½ measure sugar syrup
- ginger ale, to top
- lime wedges, to garnish

Shake the gin, orange juice, lime juice, lime cordial, bitters, and 1 dash of the cherry liqueur with ice and strain into an ice-filled sling glass. Top with soda water and slowly add the remaining cherry liqueur and Benedictine so they float at the top of the glass. Garnish with a split lemon slice and a cherry, and serve with straws.

orlando

- 1½ measures gin
- 2 dashes Chambord (black raspberry liqueur)
- 2 measures pineapple juice
- 2 raspberries, to garnish

Shake the gin, Chambord, and pineapple juice vigorously (to create a surface foam) and strain into an ice-filled old-fashioned glass. Garnish with raspberries and serve with short straws.

3

cocktails

Rum makes wonderful cocktails. It is said to date back to the early 16th century—at first it was a rough spirit that colonists drank. However, its popularity later spread to Western Europe and then throughout the rest of the world. Rum is made from the sweet juice of sugar cane, although some distilleries use molasses instead. Nowadays it is usual practice for all rum to be aged in oak barrels from anywhere between one to thirty years. There are two types of rum, light and dark, the latter being a result of longer aging and the addition of caramel. How to enjoy it? Become an exotic aficionado—taste the sunshine of the Caribbean and lace your cocktails with rum!

PIÑAcolada

- 1 measure white rum
- 1 measure Malibu (coconut rum)
- 1 measure coconut cream
- 2 measures pineapple juice
- 4 chunks fresh pineapple
- 1 pineapple leaf and wedge, to garnish

Blend all of these ingredients with one scoop of crushed ice in a blender at high speed. Serve with straws in a hurricane glass garnished with a pineapple leaf and wedge.

hotRUMpunch

- 1 cup red grape juice
- 4 tablespoons brown sugar
- 1½ cups dark rum
- 6 cups dry white wine
- 2 cups red wine

This drink is to be made for a large group. In a large saucepan, warm the grape juice over a medium heat, then add the sugar, and stir until dissolved. Stir in the rum and both wines and continue to stir. Heat the mixture but do not boil. Serve hot, in wine goblets.

CHETTA'Spunch

- 2 measures dark rum
- 1 measure undiluted black currant cordial
- ½ measure Cointreau
- ½ measure freshly squeezed lemon juice
- 4 drops orange bitters
- 1 orange slice, to garnish

Build all of the ingredients over ice in a heavy-based, old-fashioned glass. Stir to chill, garnish with an orange slice, and serve with a stirrer.

Fill a highball glass with ice and add the cranberry juice. Shake the rum and grapefruit juice together with ice, and then strain over the cranberry juice, creating a "floating" effect. Garnish with lime wedges.

westINDIANicedTEA

- 1 measure Bacardi Oro (gold rum)
- ½ measure Grand Marnier
- 1 measure freshly squeezed orange juice
- 4 mint leaves
- 4 measures freshly brewed English Breakfast tea
- 1 orange slice and 1 mint sprig, to garnish

Shake all of the ingredients (including the mint leaves—not the sprig) with ice, and strain into an ice-filled highball glass. Garnish with an orange slice and mint sprig, and serve with straws, in the sun.

CANCHANCHARA

- 1 measure liquid honey
- 2 measures white rum
- 1 measure freshly squeezed lime juice
- 1 dash soda water
- 1 lime wedge, to garnish

In a heavy-based old-fashioned glass, stir the honey, rum, and lime juice until the honey has dissolved. Then add ice, stir again, and garnish with a lime wedge. Serve with a stirrer.

SPICED raspberry DAIQUIRI

- 2 measures Morgan Spiced Rum
- 1 measure raspberry purée
- 1 measure freshly squeezed lime juice
- 1 dash sugar syrup
- lime wedges, to garnish

Shake all of the ingredients with ice and strain into an ice-filled old-fashioned glass. Garnish with lime wedges.

PLANTER'S punch

- 2 measures dark rum
- 2 measures freshly squeezed orange juice
- 1 dash grenadine
- 1 dash freshly squeezed lemon juice
- lemon slices, to garnish

Shake all ingredients with ice and strain into an ice-filled old-fashioned glass. Garnish with lemon slices and serve with a stirrer.

Hemingway DAIQUIRI (papa DOBLE)

- 3 measures white rum
- 1 measure freshly squeezed lime juice
- 1 measure freshly squeezed grapefruit juice
- 1 dash maraschino liqueur (cherry liqueur)

Blend all of the ingredients with a small scoop of crushed ice and serve in a large highball glass with straws.

melon DAIQUIRI

- 2 measures white rum
- ½ measure Midori (melon liqueur)
- 1 measure freshly squeezed lime juice
- 1 dash sugar syrup
- 6 chunks ripe Galia melon
- 2 slices Galia melon, to garnish

Blend all of the ingredients with a small scoop of crushed ice and pour into a hurricane glass. Garnish with the melon slices.

DAIQUIRI mulata

- 2 measures aged rum (such as Havana 7-year old)
- 1 measure freshly squeezed lime juice
- 1 measure dark crème de cacao
  (chocolate-flavored liqueur)
- 1 dash sugar syrup

Blend all of the ingredients with a small scoop of crushed ice and serve in a chilled goblet, with straws.

frozenMANGO&MINTdaiquiri

- 2 measures white rum
- ½ measure mango liqueur
- 1 measure freshly squeezed lime juice
- 1 dash sugar syrup
- ½ ripe mango
- 1 mint sprig, to garnish

Blend all of the ingredients with a small scoop of crushed ice and pour into a hurricane glass. Garnish with a sprig of mint.

bananaDAIQUIRI

- 2 measures white rum
- ½ measure banana liqueur
- 1 measure freshly squeezed lime juice
- 1 dash sugar syrup
- ½ ripe banana
- banana slices, to garnish

Blend all of the ingredients with a small scoop of crushed ice and pour into a hurricane glass. Garnish with slices of banana.

BATISTE

- 2 measures gold rum
- 1 measure Grand Marnier
- 1 orange twist, to garnish

Stir the liquids with ice until thoroughly chilled and strain into a chilled martini glass. Garnish with a twist of orange.

STRAWBERRY**daiquiri**

- 2 measures white rum
- ½ measure strawberry liqueur
- 1 measure freshly squeezed lime juice
- 1 dash strawberry syrup
- 4 ripe strawberries
- 1 split strawberry, to garnish

Blend all of the ingredients with a small scoop of crushed ice and pour into a hurricane glass. Garnish with a split strawberry on the rim of the glass.

presidente

- 2 measures white rum
- ½ measure dry vermouth
- ½ measure sweet vermouth
- 1 dash triple sec
- 1 orange twist

Stir all of the liquid ingredients in a mixing glass with ice until thoroughly chilled. Strain into a chilled martini glass, squeeze the orange twist over the drink, and drop in.

RUM**martini**

- ½ measure dry vermouth
- 2 measures white rum
- 1 lemon twist, to garnish

This drink is strictly for the rum-lover. Fill a mixing glass with ice and add the vermouth. Stir to coat the ice and discard any liquid. Add the rum to the flavored ice and stir to chill thoroughly. Strain into a frozen martini glass and garnish with a twist of lemon.

white**WITCH**

- 1 measure white rum
- ½ measure white crème de cacao
   (chocolate-flavored liqueur)
- ½ measure Cointreau
- 1 dash freshly squeezed lime juice
- soda water, to top
- 1 lime wedge and 1 orange wedge, to garnish

Shake the rum, crème de cacao, Cointreau, and lime juice together and strain into an ice-filled old-fashioned glass. Top with soda and stir. Garnish with lime and orange wedges, and serve with straws.

scorpion

- 1 measure dark rum
- ½ measure white rum
- ½ measure Cointreau
- ½ measure freshly squeezed lime juice
- 2 measures freshly squeezed orange juice
- 1 dash sugar syrup
- orange slices, to garnish

Shake all of the liquid ingredients with ice and strain into an ice-filled highball glass. Garnish with orange slices and serve with straws.

maiTAI

- 2 measures aged rum (such as Appleton VX)
- 1 measure orange curaçao
- ½ measure freshly squeezed lime juice
- ½ measure orgeat syrup (almond syrup)
- 1 mint sprig, to garnish

Shake all of the ingredients briefly with ice and strain over crushed ice in a large old-fashioned glass. Garnish with a sprig of mint and serve with straws.

ZOMBIE

- 1 measure gold rum
- 1 measure white rum
- ½ measure apricot brandy
- 2 dashes freshly squeezed lime juice
- 2 measures pineapple juice
- 1 measure freshly squeezed orange juice
- 1 dash sugar syrup
- 1 dash Woods Navy Rum (over-proof dark rum)
- 1 pineapple leaf and 1 orange slice, to garnish

Shake all of the ingredients, except the dark rum, briefly with ice and strain into a large ice-filled hurricane glass. Float the dark rum on the surface of the cocktail, garnish with a pineapple leaf and an orange slice, then serve with long straws.

zombiePRINCE

- 1 measure gold rum
- 1 measure white rum
- 1 measure freshly squeezed orange juice
- 1 measure freshly squeezed grapefruit juice
- ½ measure freshly squeezed lemon juice
- 4 drops of Angostura bitters
- 2 pink grapefruit slices, to garnish

Build all of the ingredients over crushed ice in a highball glass. Transfer the contents to a shaker, briefly shake, and return to the glass, unstrained. Garnish with the slices of pink grapefruit.

HONEYSUCKLE

- 1 measure Creole Shrub Rum
- 1 measure gold rum
- ½ measure freshly squeezed lime juice
- ½ measure liquid orange blossom honey
- 4 drops orange bitters
- 1 flamed orange twist, to garnish (see page 25)

Shake all of the ingredients with ice and strain into a chilled martini glass. Garnish with a flamed orange twist.

cuba**LIBRE**

- 2 measures white rum
- ½ lime
- Coca-Cola, to top

Add the rum to an ice-filled highball glass. Cut the lime into four segments and squeeze into the drink, dropping each one in. Top with Coca-Cola, stir, and serve with straws.

rum**ALEXANDER**

- 1 measure dark rum
- 1 measure dark crème de cacao (chocolate-flavored liqueur)
- 1 measure heavy cream
- ground nutmeg

Shake all of the liquid ingredients with ice and strain into a chilled martini glass. Sprinkle the nutmeg on the surface of the drink.

TRE

- 2 measures gold rum
- 1 measure freshly pressed apple juice
- 2 dashes Chambord (black raspberry liqueur)
- 1 dash sugar syrup
- 1 lime twist, to garnish

Add all of the ingredients to a mixing glass, then fill with ice. Stir to chill thoroughly, then strain into a frozen martini glass. Adjust the sweetness by taste. Garnish with a lime twist.

pale**TREASURE**

- 1 measure white rum
- 1 measure cherry brandy
- bitter lemon, to top
- lemon slices, to garnish

Fill an old-fashioned glass with ice, add the rum and cherry brandy, and top with the bitter lemon. Stir and garnish with lemon slices.

black**WIDOW**

- 1½ measures dark rum
- 1 measure Southern Comfort
- ½ measure freshly squeezed lime juice
- 2 dashes sugar syrup
- 4 drops Angostura bitters
- 1 lime wedge, to garnish

Shake all of the ingredients with ice and strain into a chilled martini glass. Garnish with a wedge of lime on the rim of the glass.

RON**collins**

- 2 measures white rum
- ½ measure sugar syrup (to taste)
- 1 measure freshly squeezed lime juice
- soda water, to top
- lime wedges and cocktail cherries, to garnish

Fill a highball glass with crushed ice, and then add ingredients in order—rum, sugar, lime. Stir, top with soda, and garnish with lime wedges and cocktail cherries on a swizzle stick.

apple-soaked MOJITO

- 8 mint leaves
- ½ lime
- 2 dashes sugar syrup
- 2 measures gold rum
- freshly pressed apple juice, to top
- 1 sprig of mint, to garnish

In the base of a mixing glass, muddle the mint, lime, and sugar syrup. Add the rum to this mixture and shake without ice. Fill a highball glass with crushed ice and strain the mixture over it. Then, top with the apple juice, stir, and garnish with the sprig of mint. Serve with long straws.

mojito

- 8 mint leaves
- ½ lime
- 2 dashes sugar syrup
- 2 measures white rum
- 1 dash soda water
- 1 sprig of mint, to garnish

In the base of a highball glass, muddle the mint, lime, and sugar syrup. Fill the glass with crushed ice and add the rum. Stir, then add a dash of soda water. Garnish with a mint sprig and serve with long straws.

FIDEL'S mojito

- 8 mint leaves
- ½ lime, segmented
- 2 dashes sugar syrup
- 2 measures white rum
- beer, to top
- 1 sprig of mint, to garnish

In the base of a highball, muddle the mint, lime, and sugar syrup. Fill the glass with crushed ice and add the rum. Stir, then top with beer. Garnish with a mint sprig and serve with long straws.

naçional

- 1½ measures gold rum
- 1 measure apricot brandy
- 1 measure pineapple juice
- 1 dash freshly squeezed lime juice
- fresh apricot slices, to garnish

Shake all of the ingredients together with ice and strain into a chilled martini glass. Garnish with slices of fresh apricot.

DISCOVERY bay

- 2 measures gold rum
- ½ measure orange curaçao
- ½ measure lime juice
- 4 drops Angostura bitters
- lime wedges, to garnish

Shake all of the ingredients with ice and strain into an ice-filled highball glass. Garnish with lime wedges.

CUBANsidecar

- 1 measure white rum
- 1 measure freshly squeezed lime juice
- 1 measure triple sec
- 1 lime twist, to garnish

Shake all of the ingredients with ice and strain into a chilled martini glass. Garnish with a lime twist.

RUMtimes

- 3 drops of Angostura bitters
- 2 measures white rum
- 2 measures cranberry juice
- 1 dash soda water
- 2 lime wedges, to garnish

Drop the bitters into an old-fashioned glass, and swirl to coat the inside. Fill the glass with ice and then pour the rum and cranberry over. Top with soda and garnish with two squeezed lime wedges.

GRENADA

- 2 measures gold rum
- 1 measure freshly squeezed orange juice
- ½ measure sweet vermouth
- ground cinnamon

Shake all of the liquid ingredients with ice and strain into a chilled martini glass. Sprinkle the ground cinnamon through a flame and on to the surface of the drink.

floridaSKY

- 1 measure gold rum
- 4 mint leaves
- 1 dash freshly squeezed lime juice
- 1 measure pineapple juice
- soda water, to top
- slices of cucumber, to garnish

Shake the rum, mint, lime, and pineapple together
with ice and strain into a highball glass over ice. aa
Top with soda water and stir. Garnish with slices
of cucumber.

T&TFIZZ

- 2 measures gold rum
- 1 measure light cream
- 1 measure freshly squeezed orange juice
- 1 dash freshly squeezed lemon juice
- 1 dash sugar syrup
- 1 dash soda water
- orange slices, to garnish

Shake the first five ingredients with ice and strain into
a goblet. Add a dash of soda water and garnish with
the orange slices. Serve with straws.

cuballini

- 1 measure white rum
- 1 dash peach brandy
- 1 dash freshly squeezed orange juice
- 1 dash freshly squeezed lime juice
- 1 dash sugar syrup
- Champagne, to top
- fresh peach wedges, to garnish

Shake all but the Champagne briefly with ice and strain into a large Champagne saucer. Top with Champagne, and garnish with slices of fresh peach.

DANDY

- 1 measure white rum
- ½ measure peach brandy
- 1 dash freshly squeezed orange juice
- 1 dash freshly squeezed lime juice
- Champagne, to top
- 1 lime twist, to garnish

Shake all of the ingredients except Champagne briefly with ice. Strain into a large Champagne saucer and top up with Champagne. Garnish with a lime twist.

tequila

4

cocktails

Tequila is made from the heart of the blue agave plant, a member of the lily family—not a cactus as commonly thought—and has become Mexico's national treasure. It's also a delight for the adventurous cocktail aficionado. At present, there are over 500 types of tequila available to the consumer, several of which feature in this section. A common misconception is that high quality tequilas and mescals have a worm in the bottle. This is not the case however, as high quality tequila would never have such an addition—it was just an American marketing ploy introduced in the 40s!

MARGARITA

- fine sea salt
- 1½ measures gold tequila (such as Jose Cuervo Especial)
- 1 measure freshly squeezed lime juice
- 1 measure Cointreau
- 1 lime wedge, to garnish

Salt the rim of a coupette (see page 16.) Shake all of the liquid ingredients and strain into the glass. Garnish with a lime wedge on the rim of the glass.

GRANDmargarita

- pinch of fine sea salt
- 1½ measures gold tequila
- 1 measure freshly squeezed lime juice
- ½ measure freshly squeezed lemon juice
- 1 measure Grand Marnier
- 1 lime slice and 1 lemon slice, to garnish

Salt the rim of a large coupette (see page 16.) Shake the ingredients with ice and strain into the glass. Garnish with citrus slices.

desperado

- ½ lime, cut into segments
- 1 tablespoon brown sugar
- dark beer, to top
- 1 measure gold tequila

Muddle the lime and sugar in the base of a large highball glass. Fill with ice and slowly pour the beer and tequila over. Stir, and serve.

PINEAPPLE&MINTmargarita

- 1½ measures gold tequila
- 1 measure freshly squeezed lime juice
- 1 measure Cointreau
- 6 mint leaves
- 1 measure freshly pressed pineapple juice
- pineapple wedges, to garnish

Blend all of the ingredients on high-speed in a blender, without ice. Transfer the contents to a shaker and shake with ice. Strain into a large chilled martini glass and garnish with pineapple wedges on the rim.

CAJUNmargarita

- 1 measure chili-infused gold tequila
- 1 measure Cointreau
- 1½ measures freshly squeezed lime juice
- 2 drops Tabasco sauce
- 1 curled red chili (see below)

Shake all ingredients with ice and strain into a large coupette. Garnish with a curled red chili made as follows. Slice the end of a chili with a sharp knife five or six times. Then leave in water for two hours. The strands will curl outward, making a great garnish.

FROZENmargarita

- 1 measure gold tequila
- 1 measure freshly squeezed lime juice
- 1 measure Cointreau
- 1 lime slice, to garnish

Blend all of the ingredients with a small scoop of crushed ice to a fairly solid, almost sorbet-like consistency. The amount of ice used in the blending determines the consistency, so practice makes perfect. Serve in a large coupette garnished with a lime slice.

frozenTEQUILAsunset

- 1 ½ measures gold tequila
- 3 measures frozen orange juice concentrate
- 1 dash passion fruit syrup
- 1 dash grenadine
- orange slices, to garnish

Blend all of the ingredients, except the grenadine, with a small scoop of crushed ice. Pour the blended mixture into a highball glass, garnish with orange slices and before serving, drizzle the grenadine over the surface.

TEQUILAsunrise

- 2 measures silver tequila
- 4 measures freshly squeezed orange juice
- 1 dash grenadine
- orange slices, to garnish

Fill a highball glass with ice, add the tequila and orange juice, then slowly drop in the grenadine which will settle at the bottom of the drink. Garnish with orange slices and serve with straws.

FROZENstrawberryMARGARITA

- 4 ripe strawberries
- 1 measure gold tequila
- 1 measure freshly squeezed lime juice
- ½ measure Cointreau
- ½ measure strawberry liqueur
- 1 split strawberry

Blend all of the ingredients with a small scoop of crushed ice. Serve in a large coupette garnished with a split strawberry on the rim.

paleORIGINAL

- 2 measures gold tequila
- 1 measure guava juice
- 1 measure freshly squeezed lime juice
- 2 dashes ginger syrup
- 1 lime wedge, to garnish

Shake all of the ingredients with ice and strain into a chilled martini glass. Garnish with the lime wedge on the rim of the glass.

easyTIGER

- 2 measures gold tequila
- 1 measure freshly squeezed lime juice
- 2 teaspoons liquid honey
- 2 teaspoons ginger cordial
- 1 orange twist, to garnish

Add all of the ingredients to a mixing glass and stir until the honey has dissolved. Then add ice, shake, and strain into a chilled Champagne flute. Garnish with an orange twist.

TEQUINI

- 3 measures silver tequila
- 3 drops orange bitters
- ½ measure dry vermouth
- 2 black olives, to garnish

Pour all of the ingredients into a mixing glass, add ice, and stir until thoroughly chilled. Strain into a frozen martini glass and garnish with two black olives on a swizzle stick.

passionfFRUITmargarita

- 1½ measures gold tequila
- 1 measure freshly squeezed lime juice
- ½ measure passion fruit syrup
- 1 measure Cointreau
- 1 passion fruit, flesh only
- 1 lime wedge, to garnish

Shake all ingredients with ice and strain into a coupette. Garnish with a lime wedge on the rim.

CANCUNcrush

- 2 lime wedges
- 2 lemon wedges
- ½ measure passion fruit syrup
- 2 measures gold tequila
- 1 measure Passoã (passion fruit liqueur)
- 1½ measures peach juice

In the base of a shaker, muddle one lemon wedge and one lime wedge with the passion fruit syrup. Add the tequila, Passoã, peach juice, and a scoop of crushed ice. Shake briefly and transfer, unstrained, into a highball glass. Garnish with the remaining fruit wedges.

vampiro

- 2 measures gold tequila
- 1 measure tomato juice
- 2 dashes lime juice
- 1 dash sugar syrup
- 1 dash Worcestershire sauce
- celery salt

Pour all of the ingredients into a mixing glass, add ice, and stir until thoroughly chilled. Rim a martini glass with celery salt and strain the cocktail into it.

TIJUANAsling

- 1½ measures gold tequila
- ½ measure crème de cassis
  (black currant liqueur)
- ½ measure freshly squeezed lime juice
- 2 drops Peychaud's bitters (herbal liqueur)
- ginger ale, to top
- 1 lime slice and blueberries, to garnish

Pour the tequila, cassis, lime juice, and bitters into a shaker and shake with ice. Strain this into an ice-filled sling glass, top with ginger ale and garnish with the lime slice and blueberries. Serve with straws.

thighHIGH

- 1 measure gold tequila
- 1 measure dark crème de cacao
  (chocolate-flavored liqueur)
- 1 measure light cream
- 3 strawberries
- 1 dash strawberry syrup
- cocoa powder and 1 split strawberry, to garnish

Blend all of the ingredients with a small scoop of crushed ice and serve in a hurricane glass. Dust the strawberry with a little cocoa powder and place it on the rim of the glass as a garnish.

border**CROSSING**

- 1½ measures gold tequila
- 1 measure freshly squeezed lime juice
- 1 measure liquid honey
- 4 drops orange bitters
- bitter lemon, to top
- lemon slices, to garnish

Shake the first four ingredients with ice and strain into a sling glass. Top with bitter lemon, stir, and garnish with lemon slices. Serve with long straws.

TEQUILAslammer

- 1 dash dark crème de cacao (chocolate-flavored liqueur)
- 1 measure Champagne
- 1 measure gold tequila

Pour all of the ingredients into a heavy-based old-fashioned glass. Instruct the drinker to cover the glass with his or her hand, bang the glass on a hard surface, and down the contents in one.

sourAPPLE

- 1½ measures gold tequila
- 2 dashes Cointreau
- ½ measure apple schnapps
- ½ measure freshly squeezed lime juice
- 1 measure freshly pressed apple juice
- 1 apple wedge, to garnish

Shake all ingredients with ice and strain into a chilled martini glass. Garnish with the slice of apple on the rim.

FORESTfruit

- 1 lime wedge
- fine brown sugar
- 2 blackberries
- 2 raspberries
- 2 teaspoons Chambord (black raspberry liqueur)
- 2 teaspoons crème de mure (blackberry liqueur)
- 1½ measures silver tequila
- ½ measure Cointreau
- 1 measure freshly squeezed lemon juice
- lemon slices, to garnish

Moisten the rim of a large old-fashioned glass with the lime wedge and coat with brown sugar. In the glass, muddle the fresh berries with the Chambord and crème de mure. Fill the glass with crushed ice. Now, add the tequila, Cointreau, and lemon juice. Stir to mix thoroughly, garnish with lemon slices, and serve with straws.

OFF-SHORE

- 1 measure gold tequila
- 1 measure white rum
- 6 mint leaves
- 3 chunks fresh pineapple
- 2 measures pineapple juice
- 1 measure light cream
- 1 mint sprig, to garnish

Blend all of the ingredients with a small scoop of crushed ice and serve in a hurricane glass. Garnish with a mint sprig and serve with straws.

baja**SOUR**

- 1½ measures gold tequila
- 2 drops orange bitters
- 1 measure lemon juice
- ½ measure sugar syrup
- ½ egg white
- 1 dash dry sherry
- lemon slices, to garnish

Shake all of the ingredients, except the sherry, with ice and strain into an ice-filled old-fashioned glass. Drizzle over the sherry and garnish with slices of lemon.

HOLDSCOCK

- 2 dashes chilled Goldschlager (cinnamon liqueur)
- 1 measure chilled gold tequila
- 1 orange wedge
- ground cinnamon

Layer the tequila on top of the Goldschlager, place an orange wedge across the rim of the glass, and sprinkle ground cinnamon, through a flame, over it. Drink the shot and then bite the garnish.

kalashnikov

- 1 orange slice
- fine white sugar
- ground coffee
- 1 measure gold tequila

Dip the orange slice in fine white sugar and then sprinkle ground coffee over it. Instruct the drinker to suck the flavored orange, drink the shot, then bite the orange.

5

cocktails

Although many people prefer to drink whiskey on its own, why not use it as a cocktail ingredient? It needs careful planning and execution but the results can be magic. So, go on, try these delicious recipes and take pleasure in a job done well. You'll find many different types of whiskey, including Scotch, Irish, Rye, Canadian, Japanese, and Bourbon. It is a barrel-aged, distilled spirit, produced from grain or malt. Scotch can only be so-named if it is made in Scotland. Bourbon is named after Bourbon County, Kentucky, where it originated. The name whiskey derives originally from the Gaelic "uisge beatha," meaning, "water of life."

sweet**WHISKY**fuel

- 1 measure chilled Scotch whisky
- 4 drops Angostura bitters
- 2 measures Champagne
- 2 measures chilled Red Bull (stimulation drink)
- 1 orange twist, to garnish

Pour the Scotch whisky and bitters into a Champagne flute, add the Champagne, and then Red Bull. Garnish with an orange twist and stir before serving.

old-**FASHIONED**

- 2 measures Bourbon
- 4 drops Angostura bitters
- 2 teaspoons sugar syrup
- 1 orange twist, to garnish

The key to this wonderful cocktail is dilution by stirring. Add the sugar syrup and bitters to an old-fashioned glass, and stir with two ice cubes. Then add the Bourbon, bit by bit, along with more ice, stirring constantly. Garnish with an orange twist and serve with a stirrer.

WHISKYmac

- 2 measures Scotch whisky
- 1½ measures ginger wine

Pour both ingredients over ice in an old-fashioned glass and stir to mix.

whiskeySOUR

- 2 measures Bourbon
- 1 measure freshly squeezed lemon juice
- 1 measure sugar syrup
- ½ egg white (optional)
- 1 cocktail cherry and 1 lemon slice, to garnish

Shake all of the ingredients with ice and strain into an ice-filled old-fashioned glass. Garnish with a lemon slice and a cherry.

cinnamonOLD-FASHIONED

- 1 ½ measures Bourbon
- 1 measure Goldschlager (cinnamon-flavored liqueur)
- 1 teaspoon brown sugar
- 5 drops orange bitters
- 1 cinnamon stick, to garnish

Pour over ice in an old-fashioned glass, stir, and serve with a cinnamon stick as garnish.

ZOOM

- 2 measures Scotch whisky
- 1 large teaspoon liquid honey
- 1 measure chilled water
- 1 measure heavy cream

Shake all of the ingredients with ice and strain into a chilled martini glass.

sazerac

- 1 measure absinthe
- chilled water, to top
- 2 measures Bourbon
- 1 measure cognac
- ½ measure sugar syrup
- 6 drops Peychaud's bitters (herbal liqueur)
- 4 drops Angostura bitters

Pour the absinthe into an old-fashioned glass over ice, and fill with water. Meanwhile shake the Bourbon, cognac, and bitters with ice. Discard the liquid in the old-fashioned glass, and strain the cocktail into it (straight up).

MANHATTAN

- 2 measures Bourbon or rye whiskey
- ½ measure sweet vermouth
- 4 drops Angostura bitters
- 1 cocktail cherry, to garnish

Stir the whiskey, vermouth, and bitters with ice until thoroughly chilled. Then strain into a chilled martini glass and garnish with a cocktail cherry on a swizzle stick.

harlequin

- 7 white seedless grapes
- 6 drops orange bitters
- 2 measures Canadian whiskey
- ½ measure sweet vermouth

Muddle five of the grapes with the bitters in an old-fashioned glass. Fill with crushed ice and add the whiskey. Stir, re-top with crushed ice, and lace with vermouth. Garnish with the two remaining grapes and serve with straws.

silkyPIN

- 1 measure Scotch whisky
- 1 measure Drambuie Cream

Pour the ingredients over ice in an old-fashioned glass and serve with a stirrer.

MINTjulep

- 6 mint leaves
- 2 dashes sugar syrup
- 4 drops Angostura bitters
- 2 measures Bourbon

In the base of a highball glass, bruise the mint leaves with the sugar syrup and bitters. Fill the glass with crushed ice and add the Bourbon. Stir well and serve with straws and a cocktail napkin wrapped around the glass.

GODFATHERsour

- 1½ measures Bourbon
- 1 measure amaretto
- 1 measure freshly squeezed lemon juice
- 1 dash sugar syrup
- 1 egg white
- 4 drops Angostura bitters
- lemon slices, to garnish

Shake all of the ingredients with ice and strain into an ice-filled old-fashioned glass. Garnish with lemon slices and serve with straws.

RHETTbutler

- 2 measures Bourbon
- 4 measures cranberry juice
- 2 lime wedges

Pour the ingredients over ice in an old-fashioned glass. Squeeze the limes and drop into the drink. Serve with a stirrer.

ALGONQUIN

- 2 measures rye whiskey
- 1 measure dry vermouth
- 1 ½ measure pineapple juice
- 4 drops Peychaud's bitters (herbal liqueur)

Shake all ingredients with ice and strain into an ice-filled old-fashioned glass.

SOLERAeclipse

- 2 measures single malt whisky
    (such as Glenfiddich Solera Reserve)
- 1 dash sweet vermouth
- 1 dash dry vermouth
- 4 drops Angostura bitters
- 1 cocktail cherry and 1 mint sprig, to garnish

Shake the ingredients with ice and strain over crushed
ice. Drop a cherry into the drink and garnish with a
mint sprig.

RASPBERRYlynchburg

- 2 measures Jack Daniels
- ½ measure Chambord (black raspberry liqueur)
- 1 measure freshly squeezed lime juice
- 1 measure raspberry purée
- 1 dash sugar syrup
- lemonade, to top
- 3 raspberries, to garnish

Shake the first five ingredients together and strain over
ice into a highball glass. Top with lemonade and stir.
Garnish with the raspberries and serve with straws.

lynchburgLEMONADE

- 1½ measures Jack Daniels
- 1 measure triple sec
- 1 measure freshly squeezed lemon juice
- lemonade, to top
- lemon slices, to garnish

Shake the Jack Daniels, triple sec, and lemon juice together with ice and strain over ice into a tall highball glass. Top with lemonade, stir, and garnish with lemon slices. Serve with straws.

AGGRAVATION

- 1½ measures Scotch whisky
- 1 measure Kahlua (coffee liqueur)
- 1 measure heavy cream
- 1 measure milk
- ground nutmeg, for dusting

Shake all liquids briefly with ice and strain into an ice-filled old-fashioned glass. Dust the surface of the drink with ground nutmeg.

bridalise

- 2 measures Bourbon
- ½ measure elderflower cordial
- 1 dash rose water
- 1 edible flower, to garnish

Shake all of the liquid ingredients together, strain into a chilled martini glass, and garnish with the flower.

APPLEcrumbleMARTINI

- 1½ measures Scotch whisky
- ½ measure butterscotch schnapps
- 1 measure freshly pressed apple juice
- ½ measure freshly squeezed lemon juice
- 1 dash sugar syrup
- 1 apple wedge, to garnish

Shake all of the liquid ingredients with ice and double strain into a chilled martini glass. Garnish with a wedge of apple on the rim of the glass.

nuttyNASHVILLE

- 2 teaspoons liquid honey
- 1 measure Bourbon
- ½ measure Frangelico (hazelnut liqueur)
- ½ measure krupnik vodka (honey vodka)
- 1 lemon twist, to garnish

Stir the honey with the Bourbon in the base of a shaker to dissolve. Then add the remaining ingredients and shake with ice. Double strain the mix into chilled a champagne saucer and garnish with a lemon twist.

BOURBONcookie

- 2 measures Bourbon
- ½ measure heavy cream
- ½ measure milk
- ½ measure mango syrup
- ½ measure butterscotch schnapps
- ground cinnamon

Shake liquid ingredients with ice and double strain into an ice-filled old-fashioned glass. Dust the surface with cinnamon.

friskyBUCK

- 2 measures Bourbon
- ½ measure butterscotch schnapps
- 1½ measures pineapple juice
- cocktail cherry, to garnish

Shake all of the liquid ingredients with ice and strain into a chilled martini glass. Garnish with the cherry on a swizzle stick.

SIRthomas

- 2 measures Bourbon
- 1 dash orange curaçao
- 1 dash cherry liqueur
- 1 dash sweet vermouth
- 1 orange twist, to garnish

Stir the ingredients together with ice and strain into a chilled martini glass. Garnish with the orange twist.

st.LAWRENCE

- 2 measures Bourbon
- 1 measure vanilla and cinnamon-infused maple syrup
- 2 drops Angostura bitters
- 1 measure freshly squeezed lemon juice
- 1 cinnamon stick, to garnish

Shake all the liquid ingredients with ice and strain into an ice-filled old-fashioned glass. Garnish with the cinnamon stick as a stirrer.

KIWIinKENTUCKY

- 1 kiwi fruit, peeled
- 2 measures Bourbon
- 1 measure freshly squeezed lemon juice
- ½ measure kiwi liqueur
- lemonade, to top
- kiwi slices, to garnish

Muddle the kiwi fruit in the base of a shaker, add the Bourbon and lemon juice, and shake with ice. Fill a highball glass with crushed ice and strain the mixture over it. Lace with the liqueur, stir, and top with lemonade. Garnish with kiwi slices and serve with straws.

OLDthymer

- 2 teaspoons vanilla sugar
- 1 drop Angostura bitters
- 2 teaspoons ginger and lemon grass syrup
- 2 measures Bourbon
- flamed orange twist (see page 25)
- 1 sprig of thyme, to garnish

Use gradual dilution to build this cocktail. In an old-fashioned glass, spoon the sugar, bitters, and 1 teaspoon of syrup. Stir to dissolve the sugar. Add some ice and 1 measure of Bourbon, and mix. Add more ice and the remaining Bourbon and syrup. Garnish with a flamed orange twist and the sprig of thyme. Serve with a stirrer.

friscoSOUR

- 1½ measures Irish whiskey
- ½ measure Benedictine
- 1 measure freshly squeezed lemon juice
- ½ measure sugar syrup
- 1 egg white
- 2 dashes Angostura bitters
- 1 orange wedge

Shake all of the liquid ingredients with ice and strain into an ice-filled old-fashioned glass. Squeeze the orange wedge over the drink and then drop in as a garnish.

GEblonde

- 1½ measures Scotch whisky
- 1 measure unoaked chardonnay
- 1 measure freshly pressed apple juice
- 1 dash sugar syrup
- 1 dash freshly squeezed lemon juice
- 1 apple wedge, to garnish

Shake all of the ingredients together with ice and strain into a chilled martini glass. Garnish with an apple wedge

4THjuly

- 1 measure Bourbon
- ½ measure Galliano
- ground cinnamon
- ½ measure Kahlua (coffee liqueur)
- 1 measure freshly squeezed orange juice
- ½ measure heavy cream
- 1 cocktail cherry, to garnish

In the base of a metal shaker, ignite the Bourbon and Galliano. Now sprinkle the cinnamon over this flame. Extinguish by adding remaining ingredients and shake with ice. Strain into a martini glass and garnish with a cherry on the rim.

HIGHLANDsling

- 1½ measures Scotch whisky
- ½ measure Galliano
- 1 measure cranberry juice
- ½ measure apricot brandy
- 2 measures freshly pressed apple juice
- 1 apple wedge, to garnish

Shake all of the ingredients with ice and strain into a sling glass over ice. Garnish with an apple wedge and serve with straws.

colonelT

- 2 measures Bourbon
- 1 measure apricot brandy
- 4 measures pineapple juice
- 1 pineapple leaf, to garnish

Shake all of the ingredients with ice and strain over ice into sling glass. Garnish with the pineapple leaf and serve with straws.

MYSTIQUE

- 1½ measures Scotch whisky
- 1 measure Tuaca (Italian liqueur)
- 1 measure Chambord (black raspberry liqueur)
- 1 raspberry, to garnish

Stir all of the ingredients with ice and strain into a chilled martini glass. Garnish with the raspberry.

FRONTIER

- 2 measures Bourbon
- ½ measure Benedictine
- 2 teaspoons Vanilla Madagascar (vanilla liqueur)
- 2 drops Angostura bitters
- 1 orange twist, to garnish

As with the Old-Fashioned (see page 96) use gradual dilution to build and mix this drink. Garnish with the orange twist.

MORELLO**bourbon**DAIQUIRI

- 2 measures Bourbon
- 1 measure Morello cherry purée
- 1 measure freshly squeezed lime juice
- ½ measure sugar syrup
- lime wedges, to garnish

Shake the first four ingredients together with ice. This drink may be served either straight up in a martini glass or on the rocks in an old-fashioned glass. Garnish with lime wedges.

toddyROYALE

- 1 vanilla pod
- 1 lemon slice
- 2 measures blended Scotch whisky
- 2 teaspoons maraschino cherry juice

In the base of a shaker, ignite a vanilla pod briefly, then add lemon slice and extinguish. Add the remaining ingredients and swirl to mix. Pour unstrained over ice into an old-fashioned glass.

KENTUCKYcreamTEA

- 2 measures Bourbon
- ½ measure dark crème de cacao
  (chocolate-flavored liqueur)
- 1 dash krupnik vodka (honey-flavored vodka)
- 1 dash Cointreau
- 1½ measures heavy cream
- 2 cocktail cherries, to garnish

Fill a sling glass with crushed ice and build the ingredients in the above order. Float the cream on top and garnish with cocktail cherries on a swizzle stick.

CLASSICirishCOFFEE

- 2 measures Irish whiskey
- 1 teaspoon sugar
- hot filter coffee, to top
- whipped cream
- coffee beans, to garnish

Pour the coffee, sugar, and whiskey into a large wine glass. Float the cream and garnish with coffee beans.

CHINchin

- 1 measure Scotch whisky
- ½ measure liquid honey
- ½ measure freshly pressed apple juice
- Champagne, to top

Shake first three ingredients with ice and strain into a chilled flute. Top with Champagne and stir before serving.

DERBYcream

- 2 measures Bourbon
- 1 vanilla pod
- 2 dashes maple syrup
- 1 egg white
- ½ measure heavy cream
- ground cinnamon, to garnish

Shake all ingredients including the vanilla pod with ice.
Strain into an ice-filled old-fashioned glass. Remove
the vanilla pod and make a spiral to garnish as follows:
wind a vanilla pod around a straw and hold it in place
for a few seconds. Release it from the straw and it
should stay in a pretty spiral shape. Add a sprinkle
of cinnamon.

lorettoLEMONADE

- 1½ measures Bourbon
- ½ measure Midori (melon liqueur)
- ½ measure freshly squeezed lime juice
- 1 measure freshly pressed apple juice
- ginger beer, to top
- 1 lime wedge and 1 mint sprig, to garnish

Shake the first four ingredients with ice and strain into
an ice-filled highball glass. Top with ginger beer, stir,
and garnish with the mint sprig and lime wedge. Serve
with straws.

brandy

6

cocktails

Cocktail aficionados will certainly enjoy making wonderful concoctions with brandy, a drink that was introduced to Northern Europe in the 16th century by Dutch traders. The name originated from the Dutch word "brandewijn," meaning "burnt wine." Today, most brandy is distilled from white wine, though red wine and other fermented fruit juices are also used. It's then aged in oak barrels for several years. Fruit brandy is usually clear and colorless and should be served chilled. Even poor quality wine can make good brandy. Although cognac is widely recognised to be the finest of all brandies, you can experiment with the different varieties used here and delight in the amazing versatility of brandy!

SIDEcar

- 2 measures brandy
- 1 measure Cointreau
- 1 measure freshly squeezed lemon juice
- 1 lemon twist

Shake all of the liquid ingredients with ice, strain over ice in a large old-fashioned glass, and garnish with a twist of lemon.

NICEpear

- 1½ measures brandy
- 1 measure Poire William (pear liqueur)
- ½ measure sweet vermouth
- peeled pear slices, to garnish

Pour all of the liquid ingredients into a mixing glass, add ice, and stir until thoroughly chilled. Strain the mix into a frozen martini glass and garnish with slices of peeled pear.

corpseREVIVER

- 1½ measures brandy
- ½ measure apple brandy
- ½ measure sweet vermouth
- slices of red apple, to garnish

Shake all of the liquid ingredients with ice and strain into a chilled martini glass. Garnish the rim of the glass with slices of red apple.

JAFFA

- 1 measure brandy
- 1 measure dark crème de cacao
    (chocolate-flavored liqueur)
- ½ measure Mandarin Napoleon
- 3 drops orange bitters
- 1 measure light cream
- orange chocolate shavings, to garnish

Shake all of the liquid ingredients with ice and strain
into a chilled martini glass. Garnish the surface of the
drink with orange chocolate shavings.

BRANDYalexander

- 1 measure brandy
- 1 measure dark crème de cacao (chocolate-flavored liqueur)
- 1 measure heavy cream
- ground nutmeg

Shake all of the ingredients with ice and strain into a
chilled martini glass. Sprinkle the surface with ground
nutmeg.

INCOGNITO

- 1½ measures brandy
- ½ measure dry vermouth
- ½ measure apricot brandy
- 4 drops Angostura bitters
- 2 ripe apricot slices

Shake all ingredients and strain into a chilled martini
glass. Garnish with two slices of ripe apricot on the
rim of the glass.

FROM**the**RAFTERS

- 1 measure brandy
- ½ measure Frangelico (hazelnut liqueur)
- 1 measure Cointreau
- 1 measure pineapple juice
- 1 cocktail cherry, thinly sliced, to garnish

Shake all of the ingredients together with ice and strain into a chilled martini glass. Float the slices of cherry in the surface foam.

FOX**hound**

- 2 measures brandy
- 3 measures cranberry juice
- ½ measure Kummel
- ½ measure freshly squeezed lime juice

Shake all ingredients with ice and strain over crushed ice into a large goblet.

big**CITY**dog

- 1 measure brandy
- ½ measure Green Chartreuse
- ½ measure cherry brandy
- 3 drops Peychaud's bitters
- 1 orange twist, to garnish

Add the bitters to a brandy balloon glass and swirl to coat the inner surface. Pour the remaining ingredients into a mixing glass and stir with ice. Strain into the balloon and garnish with an orange twist.

brandyFIX

- 1 bar spoon confectioners' sugar
- 1 bar spoon water
- ½ measure freshly squeezed lemon juice
- ½ measure cherry brandy
- 1 measure brandy
- lemon slices, to garnish

In the base of a short highball glass, stir the sugar and water together to dissolve. Then fill the glass with crushed ice and add the two brandies. Garnish with slices of lemon and serve with straws.

AVONDALEhabit

- 3 strawberries
- 1 dash sugar syrup
- 4 mint leaves
- ½ teaspoon freshly cracked black pepper
- 1½ measures brandy
- 1 dash crème de menthe
- 1 mint sprig and 1 split strawberry, to garnish

Muddle the strawberries, sugar syrup, mint leaves, and pepper in a large old-fashioned glass. Fill the glass with crushed ice, add the brandy, and stir. Lace the drink with crème de menthe and garnish with a mint sprig and a split strawberry. Serve with straws.

brandy**CRUSTA**

- fine white sugar
- 2 measures brandy
- ½ measure orange curaçao
- ½ measure maraschino cherry liqueur
- 1 measure freshly squeezed lemon juice
- 2 drops Angostura bitters
- 2 cocktail cherries, to garnish

Sugar the rim of a chilled martini glass, shake all ingredients together with ice and strain into the glass. Garnish with the cherries on a swizzle stick.

PISCO**sour**

- 2 measures pisco (Peruvian brandy)
- 1½ measures freshly squeezed lime juice
- ½ measure sugar syrup
- 1 fresh egg white
- 2 drops Angostura bitters
- 2 cocktail cherries, to garnish

Shake all of the liquid ingredients with ice and strain over crushed ice into a large heavy-based wine glass. Garnish with two cherries on a swizzle stick.

piscoKID

- 1½ measures pisco (Peruvian brandy)
- 1 measure Planter's Punch Rum
- 1½ measures pineapple juice
- 4 drops orange bitters
- 1 dash sugar syrup
- ½ measure crème de mure (blackberry liqueur)
- 2 blackberries, to garnish

Shake the first five ingredients with ice and strain over crushed ice in an old-fashioned glass. Lace the drink with crème de mure and garnish with two blackberries. Serve with straws.

AMERICANbeauty

- 1 measure brandy
- ½ measure dry vermouth
- ½ measure ruby port
- 1 measure freshly squeezed orange juice
- 1 dash sugar syrup
- 1 dash grenadine
- 1 pink rose petal, to garnish

Shake all of the liquid ingredients with ice and strain into a chilled martini glass. Garnish with a rose petal floated on the drink's surface.

APPLE**of**ONE'**seye**

- 2 measures brandy
- 1 squeezed lime wedge
- ½ measure freshly pressed apple juice
- Jamaican ginger beer, to top
- green apple slices, to garnish

Shake the brandy, lime, and apple juice with ice and strain into an ice-filled highball glass. Top with ginger beer, stir, and garnish with slices of green apple. Serve with straws.

mocca

- 1 measure brandy
- 1 measure Dark Mozart (chocolate liqueur)
- 1 measure Grand Marnier
- 1 measure milk
- chocolate shavings, to garnish

Shake all of the liquid ingredients with ice and strain into a chilled martini glass. Garnish the surface with shavings of chocolate.

dame**SHAMER**

- 1½ measures brandy
- 1 measure cherry brandy
- 1 measure Kahlua (coffee liqueur)
- 1 measure heavy cream
- 2 cocktail cherries, to garnish

Shake all ingredients with ice and strain into a highball glass over ice. Garnish with two cocktail cherries on a swizzle stick.

PETITEmartini

- 2 measures VS cognac
- ½ measure Cointreau
- 1 dash sugar syrup
- 4 drops Angostura bitters
- 1 measure pineapple juice
- 1 caramelized pineapple slice, to garnish

Shake all of the ingredients with ice and strain into a chilled martini glass. Garnish with a slice of caramelized pineapple made as follows: sprinkle the surface with fine confectioners' sugar and glaze it for a brief time with a hand-held domestic blow torch until the sugar has melted and has turned slightly browned.

sangria[TRADITIONAL]

- 1 measure Spanish brandy
- 4 measures red wine
- 4 measures lemonade
- 1 measure freshly squeezed orange juice
- orange slices
- lemon slices
- apple slices
- cinnamon stick

Pour all of the ingredients into ice-filled highball glasses and garnish with pieces of the fruit. It is best made in larger quantities for a group and best consumed sitting on a beautiful sandy beach! Try and make it two hours before serving as this will give the liquid time to be infused with the fruit flavors. Just fill with fresh ice before serving.

gage's 'SECRET' sangria

- 1 measure Spanish brandy
- ½ measure orange curaçao
- ½ measure gin
- 4 measures red wine
- 4 measures lemonade
- lemon wedges
- lime wedges
- orange wedges

Fill a highball glass with ice and add the liquid ingredients. Stir thoroughly and garnish with the pieces of fruit. This drink is better made in larger quantities and left to infuse for a while before serving.

faux COFFEE cocktail

- 1½ measures port
- 1½ measures brandy
- 1 egg
- 1 dash sugar syrup
- 2 drops Angostura bitters
- grated nutmeg, to garnish

To make this caffeine-free cocktail shake all of the ingredients and strain into an ice-filled highball glass. Sprinkle the surface of the drink with grated nutmeg.

CIDERappleCOOLER

- 1½ measures apple brandy
- 1 measure apple schnapps
- 4 measures freshly pressed apple juice
- apple wedges, to garnish

Shake all ingredients with ice and strain into an ice-filled highball glass. Garnish with wedges of apple and serve with straws.

FRENCH90

- 1 measure cognac
- ½ measure freshly squeezed lime juice
- 1 dash sugar syrup
- Champagne, to top
- 1 lime twist, to garnish

Shake the cognac, lime juice, and sugar syrup with ice and strain into a chilled flute. Top the mix with Champagne and garnish with a lime twist.

redMARAUDER

- 2 measures brandy
- 2 measures cranberry juice
- ½ measure Chambord (black raspberry liqueur)
- 1 dash freshly squeezed lime juice
- 2 raspberries, to garnish

Shake all of the ingredients with ice and strain into a chilled martini glass. Garnish with two raspberries on a swizzle stick.

COLAdeMONO

- 1-inch cinnamon stick
- 2 measures pisco (Peruvian brandy)
- 1 measure cold espresso
- 1 measure Kahlua (coffee liqueur)
- ground cinnamon, for dusting

Muddle the cinnamon stick with the pisco in the base of a shaker, add the other ingredients, shake with ice, and double strain into a chilled martini glass. Dust the surface with ground cinnamon.

henryIIIcoffee

- ½ measure Kahlua (coffee liqueur)
- ½ measure brandy
- ½ measure Galliano
- ½ measure Mandarin Napoleon
- hot filter coffee, to top
- whipped cream
- ground coffee

Add the liqueurs to a toddy glass and top with hot filter coffee. Float the whipped cream on the surface and garnish with a sprinkle of ground coffee.

bosomFORaPILLOW

- 2 measures brandy
- ½ measure Grand Marnier
- ½ measure madeira
- 1 egg yolk
- 1 teaspoon grenadine
- 1 orange twist, to garnish

Shake all ingredients with ice and strain into a chilled martini glass. Garnish with an orange twist.

APPLEcartMARTINI

- 1½ measures apple brandy
- 1½ measures Cointreau
- 1 measure freshly squeezed lemon juice
- 1 dash sugar syrup
- apple wedge, to garnish

Shake all ingredients with ice and double strain into a chilled martini glass. Garnish with an apple wedge on the rim.

BRANDYblazer

- 2 measures brandy
- 1 orange twist
- 1 lemon twist
- 1 white sugar cube

Pour the brandy into a mixing glass then add the twists and sugar and flambé the mixture. Stir while ignited until the sugar has dissolved. Then double strain the mixture into a warmed brandy balloon glass.

PLAYMATE

- 1 measure brandy
- 1 measure Grand Marnier
- 1 measure apricot brandy
- 1 measure freshly squeezed orange juice
- ½ egg white
- 4 drops Angostura bitters
- 1 flaming orange twist (see page 25)

Shake the liquid ingredients with ice and strain into a chilled martini glass. Flambé an orange twist over the drink (see page 25) and drop it in.

champagneCLASSIC

- 1 measure brandy
- 1 white sugar cube
- 6 drops Angostura bitters
- Champagne, to top

Soak the sugar cube with bitters, then add the brandy, and slowly top with Champagne. Serve with a stirrer.

LAZARUS

- 1 measure Kahlua (coffee liqueur)
- 1 measure vodka
- ½ measure brandy
- 1 measure cold espresso

Shake all of the ingredients together with ice and strain into a chilled martini glass. There is no need to garnish this potent pick-me-up.

PIERRE collins

- 2 measures cognac
- 1 measure freshly squeezed lemon juice
- ½ measure sugar syrup
- soda water, to top
- lemon slices, to garnish

Shake the cognac, lemon juice, and sugar syrup with ice and strain into an ice-filled highball glass. Top with soda water, stir, and garnish with lemon slices.

VINE

- 2 measures cognac
- 1 measure freshly pressed apple juice
- ½ measure freshly squeezed grapefruit juice
- 1 dash freshly squeezed lemon juice
- 1 dash sugar syrup
- 4 seedless grapes
- grapefruit slices, to garnish

Muddle the grapes and sugar syrup in the base of a shaker. Add the remaining ingredients and shake with ice. Strain the mix over ice into a highball glass, garnish with slices of grapefruit, and serve with straws.

PEACHbrandySMASH

- 5 or 6 mint leaves
- 1 teaspoon brown sugar
- 1 dash cold water
- 2 measures brandy
- ½ measure peach schnapps
- 1 mint sprig and 1 peach wedge, to garnish

Muddle the mint, sugar, and water in the base of a shaker. Add the brandy and schnapps and shake with ice. Strain the mix over crushed ice and garnish with a wedge of ripe peach and a mint sprig. Serve with straws.

CHAMPSelysées

- 2 measures cognac
- 1 measure Yellow Chartreuse
- ½ measure freshly squeezed lemon juice
- ½ measure sugar syrup
- 4 drops Angostura bitters
- 1 lemon twist, to garnish

Shake all of the ingredients with ice and strain into a chilled martini glass. Garnish with a lemon twist.

b&b

- 2 measures brandy
- 2 measures Benedictine

Build the two ingredients over ice and stir before serving. May also be served without ice in a balloon glass—a personal preference issue.

RENAISSANCE

- 2 measures cognac
- 1 measure sweet vermouth
- ½ measure limoncello
- 5 or 6 drops peach bitters
- 1 lemon twist, to garnish

Shake all of the ingredients with ice and double strain into a chilled martini glass. Garnish with a lemon twist.

minstrel

- 2 dashes cognac
- 2 dashes chilled vodka
- 1 dash crème de menthe
- 1 dash Kahlua (coffee liqueur)

Shake all of the ingredients very briefly with ice and strain into a shot glass.

the bes

The enticing variety of spirits available today means that it isn't at all necessary to stick to traditional bases, such as rum, vodka, or whiskey in order to produce a tasty cocktail. Experimenting with more exotic alcohols and finding a flavor to suit everyone's tastes couldn't be simpler. The art of cocktail-making will continue to flourish, as more and more combinations are discovered and enjoyed. Whether you are looking to celebrate, entertain, or relax, there is a creamy, refreshing, or fruity mix to suit every occasion, and selecting a favorite from these spellbinders won't be difficult.

NATURAL**blonde**

- 1 measure Bailey's Irish Cream
- 1 measure Grand Marnier
- ½ fresh mango or 1 measure mango purée
- 2 fresh mango slices, to garnish

Blend the Bailey's, Grand Marnier, and mango together with a small scoop of crushed ice. Serve in a brandy balloon glass garnished with slices of fresh mango. Serve with short, wide bore straws.

BATIDA**goiaba**

- 2 measures cachaca (Brazilian rum)
- 3 measures freshly squeezed (if possible) guava juice
- 1 dash sugar syrup
- 1 dash freshly squeezed lemon juice
- lemon slices, to garnish

Shake all of the liquid ingredients with ice and strain into a highball glass filled with crushed ice. Garnish with slices of lemon and serve with straws.

CAIPIRINHA

- 1 lime, segmented
- 1 teaspoon brown sugar
- 1 dash sugar syrup
- 2 measures cachaca (Brazilian rum)

In a heavy-based old-fashioned glass, muddle the lime, brown sugar, and sugar syrup. Fill the glass with crushed ice, add cachaca, stir, and serve with straws and a stirrer.

Zesty

- 2 measures Frangelico (hazelnut liqueur)
- 2 lime wedges

Fill a brandy balloon glass with crushed ice, add the Frangelico, then squeeze the two lime wedges into the drink, dropping them in as garnish. Serve with short straws.

TOBLERONE

- 1 measure Bailey's Irish Cream
- 1 measure Frangelico (hazelnut liqueur)
- ½ measure dark crème de cacao (chocolate-flavored liqueur)
- ½ measure clear liquid honey
- 1 measure heavy cream
- 1 teaspoon chocolate sauce

Blend the Bailey's, Frangelico, crème de cacao, honey, and cream with half a scoop of crushed ice. Take a hurricane glass and swirl chocolate sauce around the inner surface. Then pour in the creamy liquid and serve with straws.

PIMMS'n'GINclassic

- 1 measure Pimms No.1
- 1 measure gin
- cucumber slices
- 1 strawberry
- apple slices
- lemon slices
- orange slices
- lemonade and ginger ale, to top
- 1 mint sprig, to garnish

Fill a highball glass with ice, then add the Pimms and the gin. Put all of the garnishes in the glass and top with the lemonade and ginger ale. Finish off with the mint sprig and serve with straws.

GREENfairy

- 1 measure absinthe
- 1 measure freshly squeezed lemon juice
- 2 drops Angostura bitters
- ½ egg white
- ½ measure sugar syrup
- 1 measure chilled water

Shake all of the ingredients with ice and strain into a chilled martini glass.

MANDARITO

- 6 mint leaves
- ½ lime, cut into wedges
- 1 dash sugar syrup
- 1 measure Mandarin Napoleon (tangerine-based liqueur)
- 1 measure vodka
- 1 mint sprig, to garnish

In the base of a highball glass, muddle the mint leaves, lime wedges, and sugar syrup. Then fill the glass with crushed ice, add the liqueur and vodka, and stir. Re-fill the glass with crushed ice, garnish with a sprig of mint, and serve with straws.

loveJUNK

- ½ measure peach schnapps
- ½ measure vodka
- ½ measure Midori (melon liqueur)
- 1½ measures freshly pressed apple juice
- red apple slices, to garnish

Shake all of the ingredients together with ice and strain over ice into a large old-fashioned glass. Garnish with slices of red apple.

OYSTERroyale

- 1 small plump oyster
- Dash Creme de Cassis
- Chilled Champagne to top

Place the oyster in the base of a slim shot glass, add cassis and top with Champagne. Down in one.

ITALIANcoffee

- 2 measures amaretto
- hot black coffee
- whipped cream, to top
- 3 coffee beans, to garnish

Pour the amaretto and coffee into a toddy glass, then float the whipped cream on top. Garnish with three coffee beans, floating on the cream surface.

COFFOLOGY

- 1 measure cold espresso
- 1 measure Grand Marnier
- ½ measure Bailey's Irish Cream
- 2 orange twists, to garnish

Fill a brandy balloon glass with crushed ice and pour each ingredient over. Stir thoroughly, garnish with orange twists, and serve with a stirrer.

classAPART

- 1 measure Grand Marnier
- 1 teaspoon brown sugar
- 6 drops Angostura bitters
- Champagne, to top
- 1 orange twist, to garnish

A subtle, but beautiful twist on the original. Soak the sugar in the bitters, and place in the bottom of a Champagne flute. Add the Grand Marnier, and then top with Champagne. Garnish with an orange twist and serve with a stirrer.

KIRroyale

- ½ measure crème de cassis (black currant liqueur)
- Champagne, to top

Pour the cassis into a flute and top with chilled Champagne.

passionateAFFAIR

- ½ measure Passoã (passion fruit liqueur)
- 1 dash passion fruit syrup
- ½ passion fruit
- 1 dash freshly squeezed lime juice
- Champagne, to top

Shake all of the ingredients, except the Champagne briefly with ice, and strain into a large chilled Champagne flute. Top with Champagne and stir thoroughly prior to serving.

GRANDmimosa

- ½ measure Grand Marnier
- 1 measure freshly squeezed orange juice
- Champagne, to top
- 1 orange twist, to garnish

Pour the Grand Marnier and orange juice into a chilled Champagne flute and stir. Top with chilled Champagne and garnish with an orange twist. Serve with a stirrer.

BELLINI

- 1 measure white peach purée
- ½ measure peach schnapps
- Champagne, to top
- 1 fresh peach wedge, to garnish

Add the peach purée and schnapps to a Champagne flute and stir to mix thoroughly. Slowly add the Champagne, using a long bar spoon with a twisted stem and a flat end. Hold the spoon vertically, spoon side up, with the flat end in contact with the purée in the flute. Then pour the Champagne down the stem of the spoon raising it as you fill the glass. Stir the cocktail, and garnish with a slice of fresh peach.

ritzFIZZ

- 2 dashes amaretto
- 2 dashes blue curaçao
- 2 dashes freshly squeezed lemon juice
- Champagne, to top
- 1 rose petal, to garnish

Pour the amaretto, curaçao, and lemon juice into a Champagne flute and top with Champagne. Stir thoroughly and float the rose petal on the drink's surface.

COWGIRL

- 1 measure chilled peach schnapps
- ½ measure Bailey's Irish Cream
- 1 ripe peach wedge

Layer the Bailey's over the schnapps and serve with a wedge of peach to be eaten after the shot.

flatliner

- ½ measure sambuca
- 4 drops Tabasco sauce
- ½ measure gold tequila

In a shot glass layer in the following order: sambuca, Tabasco, tequila. Down in one.

rivieraFIZZ

- ½ measure crème de cassis (black currant liqueur)
- ½ measure Poire William (pear liqueur)
- Champagne, to top
- 2 peeled ripe pear slices, to garnish

Pour the cassis and Poire William into a mixing glass, add ice, and stir to chill. Strain into a large martini glass and top with Champagne. Garnish with slices of peeled pear on the rim of the glass.

CHERRYaid

- ½ measure absinthe
- ½ measure Wisniowka Cherry (cherry-flavored vodka)
- ½ measure sloe gin
- 1 dash sugar syrup
- 1 dash maraschino liqueur
- 1 dash freshly squeezed lemon juice
- Champagne, to top
- 1 cocktail cherry, to garnish

Shake all of the ingredients except the Champagne with ice and strain into a large flute. Top with Champagne and garnish with a cocktail cherry.

BLACKvelvet

- 2 measures Guinness
- Champagne, to top

Pour Guinness into a highball glass, then top with Champagne.

angelFACE

- 1 measure apricot brandy
- 1 measure gin
- 1 measure apple brandy
- 1 lemon twist, to garnish

Shake the ingredients with ice and strain into a chilled martini glass. Garnish with a lemon twist.

MADAGASCARfizz

- ½ measure maraschino liqueur
- ½ measure Madagascar vanilla (vanilla liqueur)
- Champagne, to top
- 1 cocktail cherry, to garnish

Build the liqueurs in a chilled flute, top with Champagne, and garnish with a cocktail cherry on a swizzle stick.

GREEKlightning

- ½ measure ouzo
- ½ measure vodka
- ½ measure Chambord (black raspberry liqueur)

Shake all of the ingredients together and strain into a shot glass. Best served for more than one person.

AMARETTO sour

- 2 measures amaretto
- 1 measure freshly squeezed lemon juice
- 1 dash sugar syrup
- 1 egg white
- 4 drops Angostura bitters

Shake all of the ingredients with ice and strain into an ice-filled old-fashioned glass.

APPLE cider SLIDER

- 1 measure Morgan's Spiced Rum
- 1 measure apple schnapps
- ½ measure cinnamon schnapps
- 1 dash lemonade
- 1 apple wedge, to garnish

Shake the rum and both types of schnapps with ice and strain into a chilled martini glass. Add a dash of chilled lemonade, stir, and garnish with a lemon twist.

LOCH almond

- 1½ measures amaretto
- 1½ measures Scotch whisky
- ginger ale, to top
- 1 amaretti biscuit, to garnish

Build the ingredients over ice in a highball glass. Stir and float the biscuit as the garnish.

REDheat

- ½ measure vodka
- ½ measure peach schnapps
- ½ measure Jägermeister (herbal liqueur)
- 1 dash cranberry juice

Shake all of the ingredients briefly with ice and strain into a shot glass.

midnightRAMBLER

- 2 measures Frangelico (hazelnut liqueur)
- 2 measures Bailey's Irish Cream

Pour both ingredients over crushed ice in an old-fashioned glass, and serve with short straws. A wonderful night-cap.

PURPLEturtle

- ½ measure tequila
- ½ measure blue curaçao
- ½ measure sloe gin

Shake all of the ingredients briefly with ice and strain into a chilled shot glass.

GREENhornet

- ½ measure Pisang Ambon (banana liqueur)
- ½ measure vodka
- 1 tiny dash absinthe
- 1 dash lime cordial

Shake all of the ingredients very briefly with ice and double strain into a chilled shot glass.

PASSION

- ½ measure cherry brandy
- ½ measure bourbon
- ½ measure Passoã (passion fruit liqueur)
- 1½ measures cranberry juice
- ½ measure coconut cream

Shake all of the ingredients with ice and double strain into a chilled martini glass. Garnish with cherries on a swizzle stick.

sweet&chili

- 1 measure Fallen Vodka (Batch 1)
- 1 measure Mozart white chocolate liqueur
- 2 strawberries
- 1 inch red chili

Muddle the chili and the strawberries briefly in the base of a shaker. Add the vodka and liqueur. Shake briefly with ice and double strain into a chilled martini glass.

BUTTERFLIRT

- ½ measure butterscotch schnapps
- ½ measure Bailey's Irish Cream
- ½ measure chilled Absolut Vanilla (vanilla-flavored vodka)

In a shot glass layer the ingredients in the following order: schnapps, Bailey's, vodka. Then down in one.

INDULGENCE

- ½ measure amaretto
- ½ measure dark crème de cacao
  (chocolate-flavored liqueur)
- ½ measure Amarula Cream Liqueur

Layer in a shot glass in the order given above (with the cream liqueur on top).

rambler

- 1 lime wedge
- 1 measure gold rum
- 1 dash Frangelico (hazelnut liqueur)
- 1 dash strawberry syrup

Squeeze the lime wedge into a cocktail shaker, then add the three liquid ingredients. Shake briefly with ice and double strain into a chilled shot glass.

MEXICANmarshmallowMOCHA

- 2 teaspoons cocoa powder, plus a little extra as a garnish
- 1 measure Kahlua (coffee liqueur)
- hot filter coffee
- 2 marshmallows and whipped cream, to garnish

Put the cocoa powder in the base of a toddy glass, add the Kahlua and coffee, then stir to dissolve. Drop two marshmallows in, and float the cream over these. Dust the surface with cocoa powder.

china WHITE

- ½ measure Bailey's Irish Cream
- ½ measure chilled vodka
- ½ measure white crème de cacao
  (chocolate-flavored liqueur)

Pour all of the ingredients into a shaker, shake very
briefly with ice, and strain into a shot glass.

TRIBBBLE

- ½ measure butterscotch schnapps
- ½ measure crème de bananes
- ½ measure Bailey's Irish Cream

Layer the ingredients in the order given above, with
the Bailey's on top.

parisian SPRING punch

- 1½ measures apple brandy
- ½ measure Noilly Prat (dry vermouth)
- ½ measure freshly squeezed lemon juice
- 1 dash sugar syrup
- Champagne, to top
- red apple slices, to garnish

Shake all of the ingredients together briefly with ice.
Strain over crushed ice in a sling glass. Top with
Champagne, garnish with red apple slices, and serve
with straws.

pure and

8

simple

Sometimes alcohol can be too much of a good thing—so none of the cocktails featured in this section contain any. Moreover, they are a great pick me up if you drank too much the night before! They're also great to offer to non-drinkers at parties. Packed full of vitamins and minerals, these cocktails taste divine and will rejuvenate and refresh the body and mind. For many of these drinks, a juicer will be required, as the majority of the recipes contain fresh fruit, vegetables, and herbs. It's really worth investing in one, as fresh fruit juices generally taste much better in cocktails than concentrated juices.

grapesGALORE

- 10 green seedless grapes
- 10 red seedless grapes
- 6 strawberries
- 1 apple
- 6 leaves fresh mint

Combine the fresh juices of all ingredients, shake briefly with ice and serve in a highball with long straws.

lemon,LIME&BITTERS

- 1 measure freshly squeezed lime juice
- ½ measure lime cordial
- 4 drops Angostura bitters
- lemonade, to top
- lime wedges, to garnish

Build the first three ingredients over ice in a highball glass. Stir well and top with lemonade. Stir again and garnish with lime wedges.

LOOSEjuice

- 2 measures freshly squeezed orange juice
- 2 measures pineapple juice
- 2 measures guava juice
- 2 measures cranberry juice
- 1 dash passion fruit syrup
- 1 dash freshly squeezed lime juice
- orange slices, to garnish

Shake all of the liquid ingredients with ice and strain over ice into a large highball glass. Garnish with orange slices and serve with straws.

virgin**MARY**

- 2 dashes Tabasco sauce
- 4 dashes Worcestershire sauce
- celery salt and black pepper
- 1 dash freshly squeezed lime juice
- 8 measures tomato juice
- 1 stick of celery, to garnish

Shake all of the ingredients briefly with ice and strain over ice into a highball glass. Garnish with a stick of celery and serve with straws.

DESIGNER**fuel**

- ½ ripe mango
- 3 strawberries
- 6 blueberries
- 1 dash freshly squeezed lime juice
- 2 measures cranberry juice
- 4 measures Red Bull (stimulation drink)
- 1 split strawberry, to garnish

Blend all of the ingredients with a scoop of crushed ice on high-speed. Serve in a highball glass with straws and garnish with a split strawberry on the rim.

ST.**clements**

- 4 measures freshly squeezed orange juice
- 4 measures bitter lemon
- orange and lemon slices, to garnish

Pour the ingredients over ice in a highball glass, stir thoroughly, garnish with the orange and lemon slices, and serve with straws.

lemonESSENCE

- 1 apple
- juice of 1 lemon
- 8 carrots
- 1 inch slice ginger root
- 6oz clover sprouts

Juice the 4 ingredients and serve chilled with a straw.

virginity

- 4 measures cranberry juice
- 1 dash black currant cordial
- ½ measure freshly squeezed lemon juice
- 3 measures freshly pressed apple juice
- 5 chunks watermelon, to garnish

Blend all of the ingredients with a small scoop of crushed ice and serve in a highball glass with straws. Garnish with whole chunks of fresh watermelon.

kiwi&bananaSMOOTHIE

- 1 kiwi fruit
- ½ banana
- ½ measure vanilla syrup
- 4 measures milk
- kiwi slices, to garnish

Blend all of the liquid ingredients with a small scoop of ice and pour into a highball glass. Garnish with kiwi slices and serve with straws.

PINEAPPLE&MINTaffair

- 6 mint leaves
- 6 chunks fresh pineapple
- 1 dash sugar syrup
- 2 measures pineapple juice
- 1 dash freshly squeezed lemon juice
- soda water, to top
- pineapple strips, to garnish

Muddle mint and pineapple chunks with the sugar syrup in the base of a highball glass. Fill the glass with crushed ice and add the juices. Stir, charge with soda water, and garnish with pineapple strips. Serve with large straws.

PASSIONsmash

- 1 passion fruit
- 1 dash passion fruit syrup
- ½ measure freshly squeezed lime juice
- 2 measures cranberry juice
- Red Bull (stimulation drink) to top
- lime wedges, to garnish

Scrape the flesh of the passion fruit into a highball glass (without ice), then add the syrup, lime juice, and cranberry juice. Fill the glass with ice and transfer the contents to a shaker. Shake briefly and return to the highball glass, unstrained. Charge with Red Bull, stir, and garnish with lime wedges.

BOOSTjuice

- ¼ watermelon
- 2 oranges
- orange wedges, to garnish

Remove the flesh from the watermelon and peel the oranges. Juice these and then briefly shake with ice. Transfer unstrained into a large highball glass and garnish with wedges of orange. Serve with straws.

mintZING

- 1-inch cucumber slice, roughly chopped
- 6 mint leaves
- 2 lime wedges
- 4 measures freshly pressed apple juice
- 1 mint sprig, to garnish

Muddle the cucumber, mint leaves, and lime in the base of a shaker. Add the apple juice and shake (without ice). Fill a highball glass with crushed ice and strain the mixture over it. Garnish with a mint sprig and serve with straws.

freeSPIRIT

- 4 measures cranberry juice
- ½ watermelon
- 8 raspberries
- ½ measure freshly squeezed lime juice
- lime wedges, to garnish

Blend all of the ingredients with a small scoop of crushed ice and pour into a highball glass. Garnish with lime wedges and serve with straws.

bananarama

- ½ banana
- 2 measures guava juice
- ½ measure freshly squeezed lemon juice
- 2 measures Red Bull (stimulation drink)
- lemon slices, to garnish

Blend the liquid ingredients with a small scoop of ice and pour into a highball glass. Garnish with lemon slices and serve with straws.

pearSTYLE

- 1 pear
- 3 ripe plums
- 1 stick celery
- 4 measures freshly pressed apple juice
- 1 dash freshly squeezed lemon juice
- pear slices, to garnish

Juice the pear, plums, and celery, and shake with the apple, lemon, and ice. Strain into a large highball glass over ice and garnish with slices of pear.

YOGIjuice

- 2 carrots
- 1 celery stalk
- ½ cup fresh spinach
- ¾ cup lettuce leaves
- 2 teaspoons parsley,
- chopped parsley sprigs, to garnish

Run all of the ingredients through a juicer and then blend the juice with a small scoop of crushed ice. Garnish with parsley sprigs and serve with wide bore straws.

FAMOUS5

- 1 tomato
- ½ cucumber
- 1 carrot
- ½ green bell pepper
- ½ cup fresh spinach
- celery salt and freshly ground black pepper, to taste
- cucumber strips, to garnish

Juice the first five ingredients and then shake with the seasoning and ice. Strain over ice into a large highball glass and garnish with strips of cucumber.

lush

- 1 cup unflavored yogurt
- 1 dash freshly squeezed lime juice
- 2 measures cranberry juice
- 4 mint leaves
- 4 strawberries
- ½ watermelon
- 1 split strawberry, to garnish

Blend all of the ingredients (except the garnish) with a small scoop of crushed ice and pour into a large highball glass. Garnish with the split strawberry and serve with straws.

health**FREAK**

- ½ cup cucumber
- 1 small potato
- 2 carrots
- 5 radishes
- cucumber strips, to garnish

Juice the first four ingredients, then briefly shake with ice and strain into an ice-filled old-fashioned glass. Garnish with strips of cucumber and serve with straws.

THYME**out**

- 4 mint leaves
- 1 cup fresh pineapple
- 1 sprig thyme
- ½ measure freshly squeezed lemon juice
- pineapple strips, to garnish

Blend all of the ingredients without ice on high-speed until herbs are well broken down. Strain this mixture over crushed ice in a highball and garnish with pineapple strips. Serve with straws.

green**PEACE**

- 3 beetroots
- 2 sticks celery
- 2 inch slice ginger root
- 3 carrots

Juice the four ingredients and serve chilled, first thing in the morning!

MONDAYflavors

- 2 measures freshly squeezed orange juice
- 1 small beet
- 1-inch cube of ginger root, chopped
- 1 carrot

Juice the beet together with the ginger and carrot. Pour into a blender with the orange juice and a small scoop of crushed ice. Blend on high-speed and pour into a highball glass. Serve with straws.

BORAboraBREW

- 4 measures pineapple juice
- 1 dash grenadine
- ginger ale, to top
- lime wedges, to garnish

Build the ingredients over ice and stir before serving. Garnish with lime wedges.

swindonCOOLER

- 6 measures freshly squeezed pink grapefruit juice
- 2 measures lychee juice
- 1 dash sugar syrup
- pink grapefruit wedge, to garnish

Shake the juices and sugar syrup together briefly with ice and strain over ice in a highball glass. Garnish with a wedge of pink grapefruit.

BERRYblush

- 6 blueberries
- 3 blackberries
- 2 teaspoons orgeat syrup (almond syrup)
- 4 measures freshly squeezed pink grapefruit juice
- 1 blackberry, to garnish

Muddle the berries and syrup in the base of a highball glass then fill the glass with crushed ice. Top with grapefruit juice and stir. Garnish with a blackberry and serve with straws.

LUXURYicedTEA

- ½ measure peach juice
- ½ measure freshly squeezed orange juice
- 1 dash freshly squeezed lemon juice
- 1 dash sugar syrup
- 3 measures cold English Breakfast tea
- 3 measures cold Earl Grey tea
- 1 mint sprig, to garnish

Shake all of the ingredients together with ice and strain into a large martini glass over ice. Garnish with a mint sprig and serve with straws. This cocktail is best made in batches and kept refrigerated.

INDEX